I0138714

OF

THE VOCATION

OF

OUR AGE

FOR

𝕷𝖊𝖌𝖎𝖘𝖑𝖆𝖙𝖎𝖔𝖓 𝖆𝖓𝖉 𝕵𝖚𝖗𝖎𝖘𝖕𝖗𝖚𝖉𝖊𝖓𝖈𝖊,

TRANSLATED FROM THE GERMAN OF

FREDERICK CHARLES VON SAVIGNY,

BY

ABRAHAM HAYWARD.

THE LAWBOOK EXCHANGE, LTD.
Clark, New Jersey

ISBN 9781584771890 (hardcover)
ISBN 9781616191023 (paperback)

Lawbook Exchange edition 2011

The quality of this reprint is equivalent to the quality of the original work.

THE LAWBOOK EXCHANGE, LTD.
33 Terminal Avenue
Clark, New Jersey 07066-1321

*Please see our website for a selection of our other publications
and fine facsimile reprints of classic works of legal history:*
www.lawbookexchange.com

Library of Congress Cataloging-in-Publication Data

Savigny, Friedrich Karl von, 1779-1861.
  [Vom Beruf unserer Zeit fur Gesetzgebung und Rechtswissenschaft.
English]
  Of the vocation of our age for legislation and jurisprudence / translated from
the German of Frederick Charles von Savigny by Abraham Hayward.
     p. cm.
  Originally published: 2nd ed. London : Littlewood & Co., 1831.
  Includes bibliographical references.
  ISBN 1-58477-189-5 (cloth: acid-free paper)
  1. Law—Germany—Codification. 2. Law reform—Germany. 3. Jurisprudence.
I. Title.

KK900 .S28 2001
340'.1—dc21   2001041396

Printed in the United States of America on acid-free paper

OF

THE VOCATION

OF

OUR AGE

FOR

Legislation and Jurisprudence,

TRANSLATED FROM THE GERMAN OF

FREDERICK CHARLES VON SAVIGNY,

BY

ABRAHAM HAYWARD.

LONDON:
PRINTED BY LITTLEWOOD & CO. OLD BAILEY.
(*Not for Sale.*)

TRANSLATOR'S PREFACE.

"When," says M. Lerminier, in the preface to his valuable *Introduction à l'Histoire du Droit,* " after completing my courses of rhetoric and philosophy, and in that state of exaltation common to young people of lively imaginations at nineteen, it became necessary for me, as we say, *faire mon droit,* with what ennui mingled with disdain did I open the five codes! To descend from my poetic reveries touching science and literature, to the numbered articles of the *code civil* and the *code de procédure,* and to have no mental aliment, but the study of dry and meagre forms without animation and without life. — This then was law! About this time, accident placed in my hands a little tract of M. de Savigny: *Of the vocation of our age for legislation and jurisprudence.* I knew a little German, and commenced a cursory perusal of it. I with difficulty recovered from my surprise: the author distinguished between *loi* and *droit*, —spoke of *droit* in a tone of enthusiasm,—made it something real, living, and dramatic; then levelled vehement censures against systems of legislation, and codes, properly so called. What, then, *legislation* and *droit* were not the same! the five codes did not constitute jurisprudence! To confirm or dissipate this suspicion, I read over again the tract of M. de Savigny; I read his other works; in the end, almost convinced by his theories, in which, however, I had a confused notion that there was something incomplete, I resolved to push my reading farther, and, with the aid of Haubold and Hugo, I succeeded little by little, *à m'orienter* in the juridical literature of Germany," &c.

I select this testimony to the character of

the tract which I now present in an English dress to those who take an interest in the philosophy of jurisprudence, from amongst a host of equally striking testimonies that occur to me, because I think it better adapted than any to tell the reader what he is to expect from the work. And I only think it necessary to add, that, even should he fail in drawing from it that degree of inspiration which leads to the composition of histories, he is not to suppose that the time he may devote to it will be lost; for he will at least become familiar with the leading doctrines and modes of thought of a school (the historical), which has had, from its formation, the profoundest jurists of Germany for its chiefs, and may boast, at the present moment, of Hugo, Savigny, Eichhorn, Mittermaier, and Grimm.*

The first edition of the work was published in 1814; the second (from which I translate) in 1828. The circumstances which gave rise to it, may be collected from the author's preface

---

* Grimm is not a professional jurist, but he has greatly promoted the historical study of law.

by all who are conversant with the history
of the times; but as this may not be universally known, I shall briefly specify the
facts. Napoleon, using his Code (to borrow
one of Savigny's expressions) as a bond
the more to fetter nations, imposed it on
all the countries of Germany, which he
had succeeded in subjecting to his rule;
thus, at his overthrow in 1814, it was in
force in parts of Bavaria, Hesse Darmstadt,
the Rhenish provinces of Prussia, the king-
dom of Westphalia, Baden, the Hanseatic
towns, and some other ultra-Rhenish provinces. The Rhenish provinces retained it, and retain it still; in the other
parts of Germany, it was almost instantly
thrown off, as a badge of political degra-
dation; and the question immediately arose
as to the best mode of supplying its place.
Thibaut, a distinguished member of the
law faculty at Heidelberg, in a little
tract repeatedly alluded to in the following pages, proposed the adoption of a code.
Savigny, in the tract before us, warmly
deprecated so hazardous a scheme, and
maintained the expediency of reverting to

that system of law which had been superseded by the French. "Le temps et la marche des événemens" says Professor Warnkönig, "ont decidé cette importante question dans le sens de M. de Savigny; comment aurait il réclamé de nouveau, en 1828, contre des innovations projeteés, dont il n'est plus question? Mais son écrit a une grande importance historique, et son influence sur la direction de l'étude de la jurisprudence est telle, que le jurisconsulte qui cultive le droit comme science ne peut s'en passer." — *Thémis, tom.* 10. *p.* 138.

A sense of what is due to the author compels me to make a remark or two on the difficulties I have met with in my task; for the translation, I regret to say, does not read so smoothly, nor convey so favourable an impression of the original, as I could wish.

A modern English writer is expected to be so pellucidly clear, as almost to save his readers the exertion of thought; he is required, not merely to use expressions from which his meaning may be caught, but ex-

pressions admitting of no meaning but one;
and our language is now sufficiently formed
to enable a thorough master of it to be thus
rigidly precise. The Germans, however,
have never yet submitted to any restraints
of the kind; and, with regard to the use of
relative terms, in particular — those un-
erring tests of accurate construction —
a very wide license is allowed, nor is it
at all unusual to find the *dieses, jenes,* or
es (this, that, or *it)* of a German writer
referring, not to anything he has actually
said or alluded to, but to something which
he supposes may have passed through the
mind of the reader a page or two back.
Then, again, their language, with all its
richness and variety, is still confessedly
unfixed,—as one of its eulogists observes,
" its capabilities are not restricted by any
literary legislation ;"* and they still indulge
themselves in a fair proportion of mysticism.
My own very limited acquaintance with
German literature is certainly not sufficient
to justify this line of remark; but my impressions are confirmed by friends on whose

* Professor Mühlenfel's Introd. Lect. p. 15.

judgment I implicitly rely. Nor am I quite certain that the balance of advantages is with us; for extreme correctness is seldom attainable without considerable sacrifices of compass and strength.

Now Savigny's style is very highly esteemed by his countrymen, nor would it be well possible, in any version whatever, for all traces of its many excellencies to be lost; but his modes of thought and expression differ so very widely from those in fashion amongst us, as to make me, as already intimated, extremely fearful of the change an English dress may have wrought in him. Some learned friends, after reading the paragraphs to which I more particularly refer, advised me to be content with a paraphrase; but I cannot help thinking, that (at least in the case of a book printed more as a literary curiosity, than for the sake of the mere matters of fact, or even of the arguments, contained in it) it is the translator's duty to stick close to his text; and that, though he may deal as he likes with inversions of language, he has no right to meddle with inversions of thought. All purely German idioms, therefore, I have carefully removed; but (with very few exceptions) I have retained the precise mode of developing the arguments throughout.

I need hardly add, that I chose the more embarrassing alternative. It is a comparatively easy task to catch the general meaning of a work, and, for a practised writer, to express it; but to render literally an author of a speculative turn, the nicest analysis of each particular sentence, and not unfrequently of each particular word, is required. There is hardly a single doubtful passage in this work, which I have not talked over with an accomplished German jurist perfectly familiar with English, and an accomplished English jurist perfectly familiar with German;* without whose kind assistance, indeed, I could not have ventured to print the translation at all. If, therefore, any vagueness of meaning, which does not vanish on due consideration, be left, the reader may rest assured that it is

* I do not mention their names, for fear of making them answerable for my mistakes.

one which I could not venture to remove ; and that, though the corresponding English expressions are adjusted with the most scrupulous care, I am probably just as much in the dark as himself.— One of the British Essayists requests of *his* friends to have the goodness to consider that there is a purpose in it, whenever they find him more than ordinarily dull — I request of *mine* to be equally charitable, whenever they find me more than ordinarily obscure.

N. B. By *the law*, unexplained by the context, is meant the law relating to private transactions. Savigny generally says *bürgerliches Recht;* but *civil* is the only English word that could be put for *bürgerliches,* and *civil* is commonly used as a synonime for *Roman* with us.

By *the Code* (with a capital letter) is meant the French Code. To avoid confusion, I have retained the German names, *(Gesetzbuch* and *Landrecht,)* of the Austrian and Prussian Codes.

1, *Pump Court, Temple,*
    June 16*th,* 1831.

PREFACE

THE SECOND EDITION.

THE first edition of the present work appeared
in 1814, at a time which can never be forgotten
by any, who, with full consciousness, have lived
through it. For years the fetters which bound our
country to the arbitrary rule of a foreigner, had been
drawing tighter and tighter, and it was plain that,
when the designs of the oppressor came to be fully
developed, our destiny must end in the annihilation
of our nationality. The momentous events by
which the foreign yoke was broken, averted this
hard lot from our country; and the feeling of
grateful joy, universally excited by this deliverance
from the greatest of all dangers, might well be
cherished as a sacred recollection by the whole
nation. Then it once again became practicable to
address the public with freedom on matters of

general concern; and the spirit that had been
roused throughout the whole country, rendered
this a more attractive and grateful task than it
would be in ordinary times. At this epoch, accordingly, a jurist of celebrity* came forward with
a proposal for framing a code for the whole of Germany, to promote thereby the unity of the Germans — an object of the highest political importance — and, at the same time, the administration
of justice and the science of law. It was expected
that the Congress, which had just then assembled
at Vienna, would be well disposed to listen to so
patriotic a proposal.

Such were the circumstances which induced me
also, in the present work, to deliver my opinion
upon this important subject. These circumstances,
as well as the high excitement of the period in which
it appeared, are discoverable in the work; and had
I now to speak for the first time on this question,
it would undoubtedly assume a very different form;
although, as to the question itself, my convictions
have not merely remained the same, but have even
been confirmed by continued reflection and no
inconsiderable experience. It might therefore be

* [Thibaut, post, p. 20. note.—TRANSL.]

doubted whether it would not have been better to bring the work, by alterations and additions, to the form in which it would probably have appeared now. But there are no assignable limits to this mode of proceeding; it might even have led to the entire suppression of the original work, and the composition of a new one. I have therefore preferred publishing an edition like the present, without any alterations at all. Nevertheless, with regard to certain passages, I find some explanation necessary.

P. 64. is upon the unsuccessful cultivation of jurisprudence in the eighteenth century, and mention is also made of the evil effects produced by a desultory and superficial course of philosophical speculation.—Many have understood these passages as condemnatory of philosophical speculation, as applied to jurisprudence, in general. To me, this is incomprehensible; for, taking the entire context, I was speaking merely of the unfortunate application of the Wolfian philosophy* to jurisprudence, and the influence of

* [Wolf, a distinguished follower of Leibnitz. His school lasted until the advent of Kant, which may be dated from the publication of the *Kritik der reinen Vernunft* in 1781. Wolf died in 1764.—TRANSL.]

a

the latter popular philosophers.* The speculations to which I allude, however, would hardly now find followers and apologists.

In the seventh chapter, a very unfavourable judgment is passed upon the latest French jurists. Now the statements comprised in it, individually taken, are quite correct; and, in the censure itself, there is perhaps nothing which requires softening; still the general impression there conveyed is partial and unjust, a highly estimable branch of the legal literature of our neighbours being passed over in silence. This partiality is attributable, partly to the strong feeling against these same neighbours, so natural at the time— partly to my imperfect knowledge of their literature; and I gladly take this opportunity of atoning, by a public acknowledgment, for the injustice I was guilty of.†

* [Fichte, Schelling, and Hegel are, I believe, alluded to. The doctrines of Hegel, as applied to jurisprudence, have been eloquently advocated and extended by Gans, the ablest amongst the present opponents of the historical school. His principal work is on the History of the Law of Inheritance.—*Das Erbrecht in Weltgeschichtlicher Entwickelung, &c.*—TRANSL.]

† In some measure, the atonement has been made already. *Zeitschrift für Geschichtliche Rechtswissenschaft.* B. 4. s. 488—490. [The *Zeitschrift* is a law journal, edited by Savigny, Eichhorn, and Göschen.—TRANSL.]

The truth is, law-learning and the branches of knowledge connected with it, had, for a long time, been much neglected in France, although, even in these, a number of young men have very recently displayed a highly honourable zeal. Practical jurisprudence, on the contrary, has there arrived at and maintains a highly cultivated state ; and the branch of their literature connected with it, deserves the highest commendation, and might be resorted to with essential benefit by ourselves. Thus, for example, the works of Merlin, the *Répertoire* as well as the *Questions*, contain genuine samples of profound, acute, judicious treatment of cases, and our practical legal literature is, in this respect, far inferior to the French. The cause of this excellence of theirs, as also of their before-mentioned deficiencies, lies, partly in the practical turn of the nation, partly in their forms of procedure, which afford scope and encouragement, in a high degree, to distinguished talent, whilst, amongst us, the judge and practitioner discharge their respective duties in little-exciting obscurity. On the other hand, I am far from attributing the smallest portion of these advantages to the code ; whatever good they have, they have despite, and not in consequence, of it. Every thing, therefore, which my work contains against the code, I must still maintain to be true. And just so with regard to the unfavourable judgment passed upon their law-schools, whose regulations certainly restrict all free development of jurisprudential knowledge in France. I say this with the greater confidence, as this judgment of mine has been confirmed by highly respectable and enlightened Frenchmen.*

P. 159. What is here said of Blondeau's mode of teaching the Roman Law, appears, according to more recent accounts, to rest upon a mere misapprehension.

P. 165— 167. What is here said on the study of jurisprudence in the Prussian universities, has, since that time, been in some measure altered. For several years lectures have been given on the Landrecht, by myself amongst others, in which I have been enabled to avail myself of the MS. materials of the Landrecht. Of late, too, attendance on such lectures, but without prejudice to the study of legal history, has even been made compulsory,

---

* What I have here said, in explanation of my partial judgment of French jurisprudence, of the circumstances under which my work first appeared, is very fairly acknowledged in a French Review, which on the whole gives a good account of this controversy.—(Le Globe, T. Y. N. 59. 1827. 18 Aout.)

and the Landrecht is directed to form one of the subjects of the first examination. Moreover, the present minister of justice * has given the public free access to these materials; some eminent jurists are already employed upon them; and thus the lively wish expressed by me (p. 112.) has been accomplished in the most gratifying manner.

In p. 175. a wish is expressed that the obstacles to communication between the universities of the different countries of Germany, might be removed. It is well known that since that time, and quite recently by the government of Bavaria, much has been done towards this important object.

The present edition contains two appendixes The first appendix is simply a continuation of the work itself, and, therefore, may properly form part of it. The same might be said with truth of another article in the Zeitschrift, the review of Gönner, B. 1. No. 17. But this article, from the occasion which gave rise to it, could not but assume, to a great degree, the character of a personal controversy , and as I find little reason, upon the calmest consideration, to retract any part of it as unjust, neither do I feel any inclination to revive, by a reprint, after the lapse of many years and the

* [Von Kircheisen, since dead.—Transl.]

death of my adversary, a controversy which originated in accidental circumstances. Certainly there is much in that review relating to the general principles of that controversy, but any one who wishes for complete information concerning it, may refer to the Zeitschrift itself.

In the first appendix there remains but one passage to which I have now any thing to add; it is the passage in which I have given a warning against the superficial use of Universal Legal History. This passage has been sometimes understood as if I wished to reject this study generally. But whoever will read it with an unprejudiced love of truth, must find such a mis-interpretation wholly inconceivable. I have really not another word to add to defend myself against this misconstruction.*

The second appendix contains the opinion of a French court on the project of the code, quoted and praised in the work, p. 80. I have reprinted it because the French collection, in which it was published, is accessible to only a small portion of my readers.

* [The author, in the paragraph alluded to, says expressly that no sort of historical knowledge is to be neglected, but that we should pay most attention to that which relates to our own laws and institutions.—TRANSL.]

CONTENTS.

I.—INTRODUCTION.

In many countries of Germany, a want, of an adventitious nature, has now raised the question as to the best mode of dealing with the law ; and thus a question, which our governments were for a long time enabled to leave unagitated, has grown into a general subject of deliberation amongst statesmen and jurists. But a more honourable motive than the mere want, has contributed to bring about this public deliberation, — the feeling that Germany, on her deliverance from oppression, is imperatively called upon by every living energy, to shew herself not unworthy of the times. It is no mark of presumption therefore, but right and proper, for every man, who has a heart for his vocation, and a clear conception of it, publicly to communicate his views ; and jurists should, least of all, be behindhand in this respect. For it is precisely in the law that the difference between the present time and the past is remarkable.

Much perversion, in particular instances, may undoubtedly still occur upon the subject, from misconception or bad intention ; but we are once
again at liberty to ask, what is proper and ex-
pedient ? The subject may again be viewed without reference to external considerations : rulers
may again act according to conviction, and place
their honour in the general weal. No one can
say as much of the time that is past. When the
code broke into Germany, and ate in, further and
further, like a cancer, there was no mention of its
intrinsic merits, scarcely here and there in empty
phrases ; extraneous motives, wholly foreign to
the proper value of the code, determined every
thing, — a state of things flagitious in itself, independently of the consideration that the object in
view was the most pernicious of all objects. Until
now, therefore, it was fruitless to speak upon the
subject. Those who, during this period, did speak
upon it, were partly advocates of the bad cause
from interested motives; partly, with inconceivable simplicity, stultified by it ; most of them
merely assisted in the undertaking, as practical
men, without adopting an opinion of their own ;
some few voices, well meriting attention, were
raised, rebuking and warning ; others, making

signs and indicating, but none with any hope of success. That once again a diversity of opinions may exist; that once again the decision can be a subject of dispute, is one of the blessings which God has vouchsafed to us; for only from this di- versity can a living and firm unity proceed, — the unity of conviction, for which our nature compels us to struggle in all matters of mind.

But there are two modes of carrying on a con- troversy; one hostile, and one amicable. We adopt the first when we find the motive and object to be bad; the latter, when we are investigating the means to objects of general good. The former would be applicable, even now when there is no longer any question of the code, should any one maintain that this is the proper time for each par- ticular state of Germany to isolate itself, that the law is a fit instrument for the purpose, and that every government should provide a separate code for itself, in order to remove, even from the law, every thing that might revive a recollection of the common national tie. This view is any thing but imaginary; on the contrary, many a government notoriously inclines to it; but a certain appre- hension prevents it from being publicly avowed at present, and I doubt whether it has ever been advanced in any work on the law. Wholly different is it with the plans, which, up to the present time, have been proposed with regard to this law; for with them, even where we do not agree, the amicable mode is possible; and this leads, if not to the unanimity of the disputants, at least to a better understanding on the whole.

Of two opinions as to the establishment of the law, with which I am acquainted, the one inclines to the restoration of the old system, * the other to the adoption of a general code for all the states of Germany. † To illustrate this second opinion, some observations are necessary here; as it must be considered in a twofold historical connection.

In the first place, it is connected with many plans and experiments of the kind since the middle of the eighteenth century. During this period the whole of Europe was actuated by a blind rage for improvement. All sense and feeling of the greatness by which other times were charac-

---

* Rehberg on the Code Napoleon, Hanover, 1814.

† K. E. Schmid Deutschlands Wiedergeburt, Jena, 1814, s. 135. Thibaut über die Nothwendigkeit eines allgemeinen bürgerlichen Rechts für Deutschland. Heidelberg, 1814. The former contends for the immediate adoption of the Austrian code, the latter for a new one.

terized, as also of the natural development of communities and institutions, all, consequently, that is wholesome and profitable in history, was lost; it's place was supplied by the most extravagant anticipations of the present age, which was believed to be destined to nothing less than to the being a picture of absolute perfection. This impulse manifested itself in all directions; what it has effected in religion and government, is known; and it is also evident how everywhere, by a natural reaction, it could not fail to pave the way for a new and more lively love for what is permanent. The law was likewise affected by it. Men longed for new codes, which, by their completeness, should insure a mechanically precise administration of justice; insomuch that the judge, freed from the exercise of private opinion, should be confined to the mere literal application: at the same time, they were to be divested of all historical associations, and, in pure abstraction, be equally adapted to all nations and all times. It would be very erroneous to ascribe this impulse, and these applications of it, to any false teachers in particular; it was, with some highly honourable exceptions, the opinion of nations. It was, therefore, not in the power of the governments to ward off all the effects; and, in fact, the mere tempering and controlling of it might often be looked upon as highly meritorious, and as a proof of internal vigour. On comparing the present time with the past, we may be allowed to congratulate ourselves. An historical spirit has been every where awakened, and leaves no room for the shallow self-sufficiency above alluded to. And although young writers often adopt a similar tone, it is no longer the prevailing one. Even in the above-mentioned plans of codes, this pleasing comparison is partially confirmed. Free from those extravagant pretensions, they are directed to a fixed practical object, and the reasonings, also, on which they are founded, are good. The lapse of this period, however, secures to us the great advantage of being able to take counsel by their experience. Those theories have successively given rise to codes for three great countries. These, and, in part, their effects, are before us, and it would be unpardonable to despise the lesson which, in the way of encouragement or warning, they are capable of affording us. In the second place, those plans are connected with a general theory of the origin of all positive law, which was always prevalent with the great majority of German jurists. According to this theory, all law, in its concrete form, is founded upon the express enactments of the supreme power. Jurisprudence has only the contents of the enactments for its object. Accordingly, legislation itself, and jurisprudence as well, are of a wholly accidental and fluctuating nature; and it is very possible that the law of to-morrow may not at all resemble the law of to-day. A complete code is, consequently, of primary importance, and it is only in case of its defectiveness that we can ever be exposed to the lamentable necessity of making shift with customary law as an uncertain kind of supplement. This theory is of much greater antiquity than the theory above-mentioned ; both have come into hostile collision on many points, but have far oftener agreed very well. The conviction that there is a practical law of nature or reason, an ideal legislation for all times and all circumstances, which we have only to discover to bring positive law to permanent perfection, often served to reconcile them. Whether there be any real foundation for this theory of the origin of positive law, will be seen in the next chapter.

II.—ORIGIN OF POSITIVE LAW.

WE first inquire of history, how law has actually developed itself amongst nations of the nobler races ; the question — What may be good, or necessary, or, on the contrary, censurable herein, — will be not at all prejudiced by this method of proceeding.

In the earliest times to which authentic history extends, the law will be found to have already attained a fixed character, peculiar to the people, like their language, manners and constitution. Nay, these phenomena have no separate existence, they are but the particular faculties and tendencies of an individual people, inseparably united in nature, and only wearing the semblance of distinct attributes to our view. That which binds them into one whole is the common conviction of the people, the kindred consciousness of an inward necessity, excluding all notion of an accidental and arbitrary origin.

How these peculiar attributes of nations, by which they are first individualized, originated — this is a question which cannot be answered historically. Of late, the prevalent opinion has been that all lived at first a sort of animal life, advancing gradually to a more passable state, until at length the height on which they now stand, was attained. We may leave this theory alone, and confine ourselves to the mere matter of fact of that first authentic condition of the law. We shall endeavour to exhibit certain general traits of this period, in which the law, as well as the language, exists in the consciousness of the people.

This youth of nations is poor in ideas, but enjoys a clear perception of its relations and circumstances, and feels and brings the whole of them into play; whilst we, in our artificial complicated existence, are overwhelmed by our own riches, instead of enjoying and controlling them. This plain natural state is particularly observable in the law; and as, in the case of an individual, his family relations and patrimonial property may possess an additional value in his eyes from the effect of association,— so on the same principle, it is possible for the rules of the law itself to be amongst the objects of popular faith.

But these moral faculties require some bodily existence to fix them. Such, for language, is its constant uninterrupted use; such, for the constitution, are palpable and public powers,—but what supplies its place with regard to the law? In our times it is supplied by rules, communicated by writing and word of mouth. This mode of fixation, however, presupposes a high degree of abstraction, and is, therefore, not practicable in the early time alluded to. On the contrary, we then find symbolical acts universally employed where rights and duties were to be created or extinguished : it is their palpableness which externally retains law in a fixed form; and their solemnity and weight correspond with the importance of the legal relations themselves, which have been already mentioned as peculiar to this period. In the general use of such formal acts, the Germanic races agree with the ancient Italic, except that, amongst these last, the forms themselves appear more fixed and regular, which perhaps arose from their city constitutions. These formal acts may be considered as the true grammar of law in this period; and it is important to observe that the principal business of the early Roman jurists consisted in the preservation and accurate application of them.

We, in latter times, have often made light of them as the creation of barbarism and superstition, and have prided ourselves on not having them, without considering that we, too, are at every step beset with legal forms, to which, in fact, only the principal advantages of the old forms are wanting, — namely, their palpableness, and the popular prejudice in their favour, whilst ours are felt by all as something arbitrary, and therefore burthensome. In such partial views of early times we resemble the travellers, who remark, with great astonishment, that in France the little children, nay, even the common people, speak French with perfect fluency.

But this organic connection of law with the being and character of the people, is also manifested in the progress of the times; and here, again, it may be compared with language. For law, as for language, there is no moment of absolute cessation; it is subject to the same movement and development as every other popular tendency; and this very development remains under the same law of inward necessity, as in its earliest stages. Law grows with the growth, and strengthens with the strength of the people, and finally dies away as the nation loses its nationality. But this inward progressive tendency, even in highly cultivated times, throws a great difficulty in the way of discussion. It has been maintained above, that the common consciousness of the people is the peculiar seat of law. This, for example, in the Roman law, is easily conceivable of its essential parts, such as the general definition of marriage, of property, &c. &c., but with regard to the endless detail, of which we have only a remnant in the Pandects, every one must regard it as impossible.

This difficulty leads us to a new view of the development of law. With the progress of civilization, national tendencies become more and more distinct, and what otherwise would have remained common, becomes appropriated to particular classes; the jurists now become more and more a distinct class of the kind; law perfects its language, takes a scientific direction, and, as formerly it existed in the consciousness of the community, it now devolves upon the jurists, who thus, in this department, represent the community. Law is henceforth more artificial and complex, since it has a twofold life; first, as part of the aggregate existence of the community, which it does not cease to be; and, secondly, as a distinct branch of knowledge in the hands of the jurists. All the latter phenomena are explicable by the co-operation of those two principles of existence; and it may now be understood, how even the whole of that immense detail might arise from organic causes, without any exertion of arbitrary will or intention. For the sake of brevity, we call, technically speaking, the connection of law with the general existence of the people — the political element; and the distinct scientific existence of law — the technical element.

At different times, therefore, amongst the same people, law will be natural law (in a different sense from our law of nature), or learned law, as the one or the other principle prevails, between which a precise line of demarcation is obviously impossible. Under a republican constitution, the political principle will be able to preserve an immediate influence longer than in monarchical states; and under the Roman republic in particular, many causes co-operated to keep this influence alive, even during the progress of civilization. But in all times, and under all constitutions, this influence continues to shew itself in particular applications, as where the same constantly-recurring necessity makes a general consciousness of the people at large possible. Thus, in most cities, a separate law for menial servants and house-renting will grow up and continue to exist, equally independent of positive rules and scientific jurisprudence : such laws are the individual remains of the primitive legal formations. Before the great overthrow of almost all institutions, which we have witnessed, cases of this sort were of much more frequent occurrence in the small German states than now, parts of the old Germanic institutions having frequently survived all revolutions whatever. The sum, therefore, of this theory is, that all law is originally formed in the manner, in which, in ordinary but not quite correct language, customary law is said to have been formed : i. e. that it is first developed by custom and popular faith, next by jurisprudence, — everywhere, therefore, by internal silently-operating powers, not by the arbitrary will of a law-giver.

This state of things has hitherto been only historically set forth ; whether it be praiseworthy and desirable, the following enquiry will show. But even in an historical point of view, this state of law requires to be more accurately defined. In the first place, in treating of it, a complete undisturbed national development is assumed ; the influence of an early connection with foreign jurisprudence will, farther on, be illustrated by the example of Germany. It will likewise appear, that a partial influence of legislation on jurisprudence may sometimes produce a beneficial, and sometimes an injurious, effect. Lastly, there are great variations within the limits of the validity and application of the law. For, as the same nation branches off into many stocks, and states are united or disunited, the same law may sometimes be common to several independent states; and sometimes, in different parts of the same state, together with the same fundamental principles, a great diversity of particular provisions may prevail.

Amongst the German jurists, Hugo has the great merit of having, in most of his works, systematically striven against the prevailing theories.* In this respect, also, high honour is due to the memory of Möser, who generally aimed at interpreting history in the most comprehensive sense, and often with peculiar reference to law. That his example has been in a great degree neglected by jurists, was to be expected, since he was not of their craft, and has neither delivered lectures nor composed class-books.

* Particularly in the Encyclopædia, Ed. 4. s. 21, 22. Naturrecht, Ed. 3. s. 130. Civilist. Magazin. B. 4. Num. 4.

III.—LEGISLATIVE PROVISIONS AND LAW BOOKS.

LEGISLATION, properly so called, not unfrequently exercises an influence upon particular portions of the law; but the causes of this influence vary greatly. In the first place, the legislator, in altering the existing law, may be influenced by high reasons of state. When, in our time, unprofessional men speak of the necessity of new legislation, they commonly mean that only of which the settlement of the rights of land-owners is one of the most striking examples.* The history of the Roman law, also, supplies examples of this kind, — a few in the free times of the republic, — the important *Lex Julia et Papia Poppæa,* in the time of Augustus,—and a great number since the Christian emperors. That enactments of this kind easily become a baneful corruption of the law, and that they should be most sparingly employed, must strike any one who consults history. In these, the technical part of law is only looked at for the sake

* [The author, I believe, alludes to the law of 1810, enacting that all hereditary tenants of lands in Prussia might, by giving up a certain proportion of them to the landlord, become free proprietors of the rest.—TRANSL.]

of the form and the connection with the whole remaining law, which connection makes this branch of legislation more difficult than it is commonly supposed to be. Of a much less doubtful character is a second influence of legislation upon the law. Particular rules, indeed, may be doubtful, or from their very nature may have varying and ill-defined limits, as, for example, all prescription ; whilst the administration of the law requires limits defined with the greatest possible precision. Here a kind of legislation may be introduced, which comes to the aid of custom, removes these doubts and uncertainties, and thus brings to the light, and keeps pure, the real law, the proper will of the people. The Roman government had, for this purpose, an excellent institution in the Prætorian Edicts, an institution which, under certain conditions, might even exist in monarchical states.

But these kinds of partial influence are not intended when, as in our times, the necessity of a code is spoken of. Rather, in this case, the following is meant :—The nation is to examine its whole stock of law, and put it into writing, so that the book, thus formed, shall henceforth be not one amongst other legal authorities, but that all others which have been hitherto in force, shall be in force no longer. The first question, therefore, is, where are the materials for this code to come from ? According to a theory already mentioned, it has been maintained by many, that these are to be supplied by the universal law of nature, without reference to any thing existing. But those who had to do with the execution of such plans, or were otherwise acquainted with practical law, have laid no stress upon this extravagant and wholly groundless theory; and it is unanimously agreed that the existing law is to be laid down with merely such alterations and improvements as might be thought necessary on grounds of expediency. That this was the prevalent opinion when the new codes were framed, will appear hereafter. The substance of a code would, accordingly, be two-fold; it would be composed partly of the existing law, and partly of new provisions. So far as the last are concerned, their occurrence on the occasion of a code, is obviously a matter of accident; they might have been proposed singly at any other time, and, what is more, there might be no want of them, at the time the code was formed. In Germany, in particular, these new provisions would often be but apparently new, since that which was new in one state might have been already in force in another ; so that the question would relate, not to new laws, but to already existing laws of kindred nations, with a mere change of jurisdiction. Not, therefore, to confuse our inquiry, we will lay new laws entirely aside, and look only to the essentials of the code. In this case we must consider the code as the exposition of the aggregate existing law, with exclusive validity conferred by the state itself.

That we should consider this last as essential in an undertaking of the kind, is natural in times so fruitful in writing as ours ; when, with such a number of authors and such a rapid succession of books and authorities, no particular book can preserve a predominant and lasting influence otherwise than through the authority of the state. In fact, however, it may well be thought that a work of the kind might be accomplished by private jurists, without requisition or confirmation on the part of the state. This was often the case with the old German law, and we should have a good deal of trouble to make our forefathers understand that difference between a law book, as a private production, and a real code, which we consider so natural and necessary. For the present, however, we have only to do with the notion peculiar to our times. Nevertheless it is clear, that this difference consists merely in the originating cause and the confirmation on the part of the state, not in the nature of the work itself, for this in every case is wholly technical, and as such belongs to the jurists ; since, as regards the substance of the code we are supposing, the political element of the law has long worked itself out, and there is nothing to do but to discriminate and expound the result, which is the peculiar function of technical jurisprudence.

The requisites of such a code, and the expectations from it, are of two kinds. With regard to the condition of the law itself, the highest degree of precision is to be looked for, and, at the same time, the highest degree of uniformity in the application. The limits of its jurisdiction are to be more clearly defined and regulated, since a general national law is to replace a varying customary law. We here confine ourselves to the first benefit, as the second will be best discussed further on, in particular application to Germany.

That this first benefit depends upon the excellence of the execution, must be obvious to all, and, therefore, in this respect, it is just as possible to lose as to gain. Well deserving of consideration is what Bacon, from the magnitude of his intellect and his experience, said of a work of the kind.* He is of opinion, that it should never be engaged in without a pressing necessity, and even then with particular care of the legal authorities in force; by, in the first place, the scrupulous adoption of every thing that is applicable in them, and, secondly, by their being preserved and constantly consulted. Above all, he says, the work should only be undertaken in times which in civilization and knowledge surpass the preceding, for it would be truly lamentable were the productions of former times to be mutilated by the ignorance of the present.† It is not difficult to say what is here required : the existing law, which is not to be changed, but retained, must be thoroughly understood and properly expressed. *That* (the understanding of it) concerns the substance, *this* (the expression) the form.

---

* Baco de Fontibus Juris. Aphor. 59—64. De Aug. Scient. L. 8. c. 3.

† Aph. 64. Optandum esset, ut hujus modi legum instauratio illis temporibus suscipiatur quæ antiquioribus, quorum opera et acta tractant, literis et rerum cognitione præstiterint. . . . Infelix res namque est, cum ex judicio et delectu ætatis minus prudentis et eruditæ antiquorum opera mutilantur et recomponuntur."

As regards the substance, the most important and difficult part is the completeness of the code, and upon this point we have only fully to comprehend the following proposition, in which all agree.

The code, then, as it is intended to be the only law-authority, is actually to contain, by anticipation, a decision for every case that may arise. This has been often conceived, as if it were possible and advantageous to obtain, by experience, a perfect knowledge of the particular cases, and then to decide each by a corresponding provision of the code. But whoever has considered law-cases attentively, will see at a glance that this undertaking must fail, because there are positively no limits to the varieties of actual combinations of circumstances. In all the new codes, indeed, all appearance of an attempt to obtain this material perfection has been given up, without, however, establishing any thing in its stead. But there is certainly a perfection of a different kind, which may be illustrated by a technical expression of geometry. In every triangle, namely, there are certain data, from the relations of which all the rest are necessarily deducible : thus, given two sides and the included angle, the whole triangle is given. In like manner, every part of our law has points by which the

rest may be given : these may be termed the leading axioms. To distinguish these, and deduce
from them the internal connection, and the precise
degree of affinity which subsist between all juridical notions and rules, is amongst the most difficult of the problems of jurisprudence. Indeed,
it is peculiarly this which gives our labours the
scientific character. If then the code be formed in a time which is unequal to this art, the
following evils are inevitable: The administration of justice is ostensibly regulated by the
code, but really by something else, external to
the code, acting as the true dominant authority.
This false appearance, however, is productive of
the most disastrous effects. For the code, by its
novelty, its connection with the prevailing notions
of the age, and its external influence, will infallibly attract all attention to itself, away from the real
law-authority; so that the latter, left in darkness
and obscurity, will derive no assistance from the
moral energies of the nation, by which alone it
can attain to a satisfactory state. That this is
no groundless apprehension, will appear further
on when we come to treat of the new codes: and
it will be seen that not only the substance itself,
but the very notion and general nature of this

true governing source of law is misunderstood,
as it then appears under the most opposite names,
sometimes as natural law (*Naturrecht*), sometimes
as *jurisprudence*, sometimes as analogical law.
If to this imperfect knowledge of the leading principles, be added the abovementioned aim at material completeness, particular decisions unnoticed by
the framers, will be constantly crossing and contra-
dicting each other, which will gradually come to
light by practice only, and, in the case of a bad administration of justice, not even by that.* This
result would be clearly inevitable, so far as cotem-
poraries are concerned, were an age, without being
fully qualified, to fix its legal notions by legislative
authority in this manner; but the effect of it would
be no less injurious to succeeding times. For
if, in these, circumstances should be favourable
for a revision of the law, nothing would be
more conducive to the end in view than the
being extensively connected with preceding in-

---

* Hugo, Naturrecht, S. 130. N. 7. " Were all law questions
to be decided by the higher judicial authorities, the decisions
would be so numerous that it would hardly be possible to
know them all; and for the undecided cases, of which no
small number are sure to remain, there would be but the
more contradictory analogies."

telligent times ; but the code now stands between, impeding and throwing difficulties in the way of this connection on all sides. Besides, in the partial dealing with an established positive law, there is the risk of being overwhelmed by mere texts, and every sort of relief must, on the other hand, be very welcome : an imperfect code, however, more than any thing else, must confirm the supremacy of this dead spiritless mode of treating the law.

But, besides the substance, the form of the code must be taken into consideration, for the framer may have fully studied the law on which he is at work, and his production may, notwithstanding, fail of its end, if he have not withal the art of exposition. What this exposition ought to be, is better shown by instances of successful or unsuccessful application, than by general rules. It is commonly required that the language of the law should be particularly distinguished by brevity. Certainly brevity may be extremely effective, as is clear from the examples of the Roman Decrees and Edicts. But there is also a dry, inexpressive brevity, adopted by him who does not understand the use of language as an instrument, and which remains wholly ineffective ; numerous examples of it are to be found in the laws and records of the middle ages. On the other hand, diffuseness in law authorities may be very exceptionable, nay, wholly intolerable, as in many of the constitutions of Justinian, and in most of the novels of the Theodosian Code; but there is also an intelligent and very effective diffuseness, and this is discernible in many parts of the Pandects.

Putting together what has been said above concerning the requisites of a really good code, it is clear that very few ages will be found qualified for it. Young nations, it is true, have the clearest perception of their law, but their codes are defective in language and logical skill, and they are generally incapable of expressing what is best, so that they frequently produce no individual image, whilst their matter is in the highest degree individual. The laws of the middle ages, already quoted, are examples of this; and had we the twelve tables complete before us, we should probably find something of the sort, only in a less degree. In declining ages, on the other hand, almost every thing is wanting — knowledge of the matter, as well as language. There thus remains only a middle period; that which, (as regards the law, although not necessarily in any other respect,) may

be accounted the summit of civilization. But
such an age has no need of a code for itself: it
would merely compose one for a succeeding and
less fortunate age, as we lay up provisions for
winter. But an age is seldom disposed to be so
provident for posterity.

IV.—ROMAN LAW.

THESE general views of the origin of law and of
codes will be rendered clearer and more convinc-
ing by being applied to the Roman and the German law.

The advocates of the Roman law have not unfrequently placed its principal value in its con-
taining the eternal rules of justice in peculiar pu-
rity, and thus being entitled to be itself considered
a law of nature sanctioned as positive law. On looking closer, the larger part will appear to be little better than narrowness and subtlety, and our admiration is almost entirely confined to its theory of contracts; deduct the Stipulations and some other su-
perstitious forms, and the excellence of the remainder

of this law, is, beyond measure, great ; nay, it may well be termed, *l'expression des sentimens mis par Dieu même dans le cœur des hommes.* But this very remainder of the Roman law, so cited for its real excellence, is of so general a nature, that it might have been discovered by plain good sense, without any juridical cultivation ; and for so slight a gain it is not worth while to invoke the laws and lawyers of two thousand years to help us. Let us take a somewhat nearer view of the characteristics of the Roman law. That it is characterised by something more than is intimated above, must have been already anticipated from its being the only law of a great people, who have had a long political existence, and enjoyed a wholly national undisturbed development ; and, moreover, from its having been at all times cherished with marked affection by them.

If, in the first place, we consider the juridical works of Justinian, consequently, that form in which the Roman law has come down to modern Europe, we cannot but remark a season of decline in them. The nucleus of these codes is a

* Motifs de la Loi du 3 Sept. 1807. By Bigot Preameneu.

compilation from the works of a classical age, which must now be regarded as lost and irrecoverable, and Justinian himself does not conceal this. This classical age, therefore, the age of Papinian and Ulpian, is that to which we have now to look, and we shall endeavour to give a sketch of the character and method of these jurists.

It has been shown above (p. 38.) that, in our science, every thing depends upon the possession of the leading principles, and it is this very possession which constitutes the greatness of the Roman jurists. The notions and axioms of their science do not appear to have been arbitrarily produced; these are actual beings, whose existence and genealogy have become known to them by long and intimate acquaintance. For this reason their whole mode of proceeding has a certainty which is found no where else, except in mathematics; and it may be said, without exaggeration, that they calculate with their notions. But this method is by no means the exclusive peculiarity of one or a few great writers; on the contrary, it is common to all, and although a very different measure of felicitous application falls to the lot of each, still the method is universally the same. Indeed, had we their works complete before us, we should discover in them much less individuality than in any other literature; they all co-operate, as it were, in one and the same great work; and the idea upon which the compilation of the Pandects is based, is, therefore, not to be altogether rejected. How deep, amongst the Roman jurists, the foundation of this community of scientific attainments is laid, is proved by the fact of their placing little value in the external means of this community; thus, for example, their definitions are, for the most part, very imperfect, without in the least affecting the precision and certainty of their notions. But, on the other hand, they have a much more important and less arbitrary means at command, an admirable technical language, so exactly harmonising with their science, that the two appear to form one indissoluble whole. With these advantages, however, a decisive partial tendency might well consist; for law has no self-dependent existence; on the contrary, its essence is the life of man itself, viewed on one particular side. If, then, the science of law be separated from this its object, the scientific energy will be able to advance in its partial course without being accompanied by any corresponding view of legal relations; the science may then attain to a high degree of formal perfection, and yet be deficient in all proper reality. But this is the very point of view in which the method of the Roman jurists appears to the greatest advantage. If they have a case to decide, they proceed upon the liveliest perception of it; and we see the whole relation, formed and modified, step by step before our eyes. It is as if this very case were the starting point from which the whole system was to spring. Thus, properly speaking, their theory and practice are the same; their theory is framed for immediate application, and their practice is uniformly ennobled by scientific treatment. They see in every principle a case of application, in every case the rule by which it is to be decided; and in the ease with which they pass from generals to particulars, and back again from particulars to generals, their mastery is undeniable. And in finding and applying the law in this manner, their peculiar excellence consists: unlike the German judges of old, in this respect — that their art is, at the same time, adapted to the perception and communication of science, without however losing the palpableness and vigour which are ordinarily peculiar to early times.

This highly cultivated state of jurisprudence

amongst the Romans at the beginning of the third
century of the Christian æra, is so well worthy of
note, that we must also pay some attention to its
history. It would be very wrong to regard it as the
pure creation of a highly favoured age, unconnected
with the preceding. On the contrary, the materials
of their science were handed down to the jurists of
this time, a great part of them even from the time
of the free republic. But not only these materials, but that admirable method itself, had root
in the time of freedom. What, indeed, made
Rome great, was the quick, lively, political spirit, which made her ever ready so to renovate
the forms of her constitution, that the new merely
ministered to the development of the old,—a judicious mixture of the adhesive and progressive
principles. This spirit was equally operative in
the constitution and the law ; but, in the former,
it was extinguished before the end of the republic, whilst, in the latter, it might still operate
for centuries to come, because the same causes of
corruption did not exist in it as in the constitution.
In the law, consequently, the general Roman character was strongly marked,—the holding fast by
the long-established, without allowing themselves

to be fettered by it, when it no longer harmonised
with a new popular prevailing theory. For this reason the history of the Roman law, down to the classical age, exhibits every where a gradual, wholly-
organic development. If a new form is framed, it
is immediately bound up with an old established
one, and thus participates in the maturity and fixedness of the latter. This is the meaning of a fiction
of the highest importance with regard to the development of the Roman law, and often laughably
mistaken by the moderns : thus, the *bonorum pos-
sessio* with *hereditas*, the *publicana actio* with the
rei vindicatio, the *actiones utiles* with the *directæ*.
And as their juridical notions advanced steadily
and uninterruptedly in this manner from the greatest simplicity to the most complicated and artificial
state, the most complete command of their matter
was, even in more recent times, attainable by
the Roman jurists ; which we marvel at in them.
Just as it has been observed above, that jurisprudence in its classical days was common to the
jurists in general,—in like manner do we now per-
ceive a similar community between the most different ages, and we are compelled to ascribe that
juridical genius to which the excellence of the
Roman law is attributable, not to one particu-

D

lar age, but to the nation in general. But if we look to scientific cultivation, by which alone a lasting influence on other nations and times could be secured to the Roman law, we must assign the first rank to the age of Papinian and Ulpian ; and were any juridical works of the time of Cicero or Augustus extant, it would not be easy to mistake their incompleteness in comparison with the age alluded to, however valuable an addition to our knowledge even they might be.

From this representation it is plain, that the Roman law, like customary law, has formed itself almost entirely from within; and the more detailed history of it shows how little, on the whole, express legislation affected it, so long as it continued in a living state. Even with regard to what has been said above of the necessity for a code, the history of the Roman law is exceedingly instructive. So long as the law was in active progression, no code was discovered to be necessary, not even at the time when circumstances were most favourable for it. For in the times of the classical jurists, there would have been no difficulty in framing an excellent code. The three most celebrated jurists, too—Papinian, Ulpian and Paulus,—were *præfecti prætorio*. These assuredly were wanting neither

in interest for the law nor in power to procure
the formation of a code, had they deemed it advantageous or necessary; yet we find no trace of
such an experiment. But when, at an earlier
period, Cæsar, in the consciousness of his power
and of the corruption of the age, resolved on being
absolute in Rome, he is said to have formed
the conception of a code in our meaning of the
term.* And when, in the sixth century, all intellectual life was dead, the wrecks of better times
were collected to supply the demand of the moment. Thus, within a very short period, several
compilations of the Roman law were formed; the
Edict of Theodoric, the Breviarium of Alaric, the
Responsiones Papiani, and the legal productions
of Justinian. Hardly would works on the Roman
law have been preserved, but for these compilations; and hardly would the Roman law have
found entrance into modern Europe, had not Justinian's works been amongst them; in which alone,
of all these, the spirit of the Roman law is dis-

---

* Suetonius, Cæsar, c. 44. Jus civile ad certum modum
redigere, atque ex immensâ diffusâque legum copiâ, optima
quæque et necessaria in paucissimos conferre libros.

cernible. The idea of these codes, however, was evidently suggested only by the extreme decay of the law.

As to the value of the substance of the Roman law, there may be many different opinions, but as to its superiority in juridical method, all are undoubtedly unanimous who have a voice in the matter. But such a voice can only be allowed to those who read the sources of the Roman law without prejudice, and in a scientific spirit. Those who know it only from compendiums or lectures,—consequently, at second hand — even though they may have made occasional references, have no voices; every opinion is plausible in their eyes, amongst others, that of an excellent French orator. He maintains, that the Roman law, in the time of the old jurists, was composed of a countless number of particular decisions and rules, which a life would have been insufficient to comprehend ; that under Justinian, however, *la legislation Romaine sortit du chaos,* whose work was the least incomplete, till, in the code Napoleon, a perfect one appeared.

* Motifs de la Loi du 3d Sep. 1807, prefixed to the editions of the code since 1807, by Bigot Preameneu.

V.—CIVIL LAW IN GERMANY.

Up to a very recent period a uniform system of law was in practical operation throughout the whole of Germany under the name of the common law, more or less modified by the provincial laws, but no where altogether without force. The principal sources of this common law were the law-books of Justinian, the mere application of which to Germany had of itself already introduced important modifications. To this common law, the scientific activity of the German jurists had been always principally devoted. But it is this very foreign element of our law which has long occasioned bitter complaints. The Roman law, it is said, has deprived us of our nationality, and nothing but the exclusive attention paid to it by our jurists, has hindered our indigenous law from attaining to an equally independent and scientific condition. Complaints of this kind have a degree of hollowness and groundlessness about them, insomuch as they assume that to be accidental and arbitrary, which would never have come to pass, or, at any rate, would never have endured, without some internal necessity. Besides, an exclusive national development, like that of the ancients, is not generally to be met with in the course, which nature has indicated to the moderns. As the religion of nations is not peculiarly their own, and their literature as little free from the most powerful external influence, — upon the same principle, their having also a foreign and general system of law, does not appear unnatural. Nay, not merely was this influence upon civilization and literature principally foreign, but in a great measure Roman, just as Roman as the before-mentioned influence upon our law. But there is another radical mistake in this theory. Even without the intermixture of the Roman law, an undisturbed progressive formation of German law would have been impossible, all the requisites being wanting, which had so much favoured the law in Rome. Amongst these, must first be reckoned the unmoved locality; Rome itself, the original state, having remained its focus till the downfall of the Western Empire; whilst the German races emigrated — conquered and were conquered by turns — so that the law was shared amongst them all, but found no where a permanent seat, still less a common centre. Then, from an early period, the Germanic nations have experienced revolutions of so sweeping a character, as are not to be paralleled in the whole history of Rome. For the very changes in the constitution under Augustus and Constantine had no immediate effect upon the law, and left even some fundamental notions of public law, as, for example, that of the Civitas, untouched. In Germany, on the contrary, as soon as the feudal system was completely established, nothing peculiar to the old race of people was left; every thing, even to forms and names, had undergone a radical change, and this entire revolution was already decided, when the Roman law was introduced.

The importance of the Roman law as an example of juridical method, has been shewn in a former chapter; historically, also, it is now of great importance to Germany, on account of its relation to the common law. It is a palpable mistake to limit this historical importance of the Roman law to the cases immediately decided by it. Not only is there in the provincial laws themselves, much law purely Roman, and only intelligible in its original Roman context; but even in those parts where its decisions have been designedly passed by, it has

often decided the interpretation and execution of
the newly introduced law, so that the question
which ought to be solved by this new law, cannot
be understood without the Roman law. This historical importance, however, the Roman law shares
with the German law, which is every where preserved in the provincial laws, so that these would
remain unintelligible without reference to the common source.

Of this extremely complicated state of the
sources of law in Germany, arising from the connection of the common law (very complicated in
itself) with the provincial laws, the loudest complaints have been raised. Those which relate to the
study, will be more in place further on; but some
concern the administration of the law itself.

In the first place, the excessive duration of lawsuits in many countries of Germany, is said to
have been occasioned by it. No one can deny
this evil to exist, or treat it as insignificant; but
it is really paying too high a compliment to the
judges in such countries, to believe that so
much time is devoted to the anxious consideration of difficult points. They are aided, in such
matters, by the first compendium or manual that
comes to hand : badly, perhaps, but with no more

expenditure of time than by the best of codes.
In many countries, this evil is attributable to
faulty forms of proceeding, and the reform of
these is one of the most pressing necessities; the
sources of the law are guiltless of it. That this is the
case, every unprejudiced person, who has studied
the forms attentively, will allow. The experience
of particular countries is to the same effect : thus,
for example, in Hesse, the administration of justice
was long ago both good and speedy, although common law and provincial law there stood in precisely
the same relation to each other, as in the countries
in which suits are interminable.

In the second place, the great diversity of the
provincial laws is complained of; and this com-
plaint is not confined to the differences between
different German states; for often, even in the
same country, provinces and towns have systems
peculiar to themselves. That the administration
of justice is impaired and intercourse impeded by
this diversity, has been often asserted; but experience is silent upon the point, and the true
ground is probably different. It is to be found in
the indescribable power, which the bare idea of
uniformity has so long exercised in all directions
throughout Europe; a power, the abuse of which

we were formerly cautioned against by Montesquieu.* It is well worth the trouble to take a closer view of this uniformity in this particular application.

The most important argument urged in favour of the uniformity of the law, is, that our love for our common country is enhanced by it, but weakened by a multiplicity of particular laws. If this supposition be well founded, every German of good feeling will wish that Germany may have throughout the same system of law. But this very supposition is now the subject of discussion.

The well-being of every organic being, (consequently of states,) depends on the maintenance of an equipoise between the whole and its parts — on each having its due. For a citizen, a town, a province to forget the state to which they belong, is a very common phenomenon, and every one will regard this as an unnatural and morbid state of things. But for this very reason a lively affection for the whole can only proceed from the thorough participation in all particular relations ; and he only who takes good care of his own family, will be a truly good citizen. It is, therefore, an error to sup-

* Montesquieu, XXIX. 18.

pose that the common weal would gain new life by
the annihilation of all individual relations. Were it
possible to generate a peculiar corporate spirit
in every class, every town, nay, every village, the
common weal would gain new strength from this
heightened and multiplied individuality. When,
therefore, the influence of law on the love of country, is the question, the particular laws of particular provinces and states are not to be regarded as
obstacles. In this point of view, the law merits
praise, in so far as it falls in, or is adapted to fall in,
with the feelings and consciousness of the people ;
blame, if, like an uncongenial and arbitrary thing,
it leaves the people without participation. That,
however, will be oftener and more easily the case
with the distinct systems of particular districts,
although it certainly is not every municipal law
that will be truly popular.

Indeed, for this political end, no state of law
appears more favourable than that which was
formerly general in Germany : great variety and
individuality in particulars, but with the common
law for the general foundation, constantly remind-
ing all the Germanic nations of their indissoluble
unity. The most pernicious, however, in this
point of view, is the light and capricious alteration

of law ; and even were uniformity and fitness attainable by change, the advantage would not be worth naming in comparison with the political disadvantage just alluded to. That which is thus constructed by men's hands before our eyes, will always hold a very different place in popular estimation from that which has not so plain and palpable an origin ; and when we, in our praiseworthy zeal, inveigh against this decision as a blind prejudice, we ought not to forget that all faith in, and feeling for, that which is not on a level with us, but more exalted than we, depends upon the same kind of spirit. This consideration might well lead us to doubt of the impropriety of the decision.*

* Compare what Rehberg, in speaking of the Code Napoleon (s. 33. &c.), says of the uniformity of the law, as well as of the important consequences of the entire change of the law, s. 57, &c.

VI.—OUR VOCATION FOR LEGISLATION.

THE grounds upon which the necessity of a code for Germany is usually rested, have been spoken of in the preceding chapter; we have now to consider the capacity for the undertaking. Should there be any deficiency in this respect, our condition, which we are anxious to improve, would necessarily be deteriorated by a code.

Bacon required that the age in which a code should be formed, should excel preceding ages in intelligence, from which it follows, as a necessary conclusion, that this capacity must have been denied to many an age, which, in other respects, may be regarded as in a high state of cultivation. Very recently, the opponents of the Roman law have not unfrequently laid particular stress upon such arguments as the following : — Reason is common to all nations and ages alike, and as we have, moreover, the experience of former times to resort to, all that we do must infallibly be better than all that has been done before.— But even this opinion, that every age has a vocation for every thing, is a prejudice of the most dangerous kind. In the fine arts we are obliged to acknowledge the contrary ; why are we unwilling to make the same admission, with respect to the government and the law ?

If we examine the expectations of unprofessional men from a code, these will be found to vary with the objects of law ; and here, also, the twofold element of all law, which I have termed the political and the technical, is manifest. In some of these objects they take an immediate lively interest ; others they give up, as indifferent matters of juridical technicality. The former is more the case in family law ; the latter in property law, mostly in its general fundamental principles.* We will take, as representatives of these different kinds of objects, *marriage* and *property ;* what is about to be said of them is to be taken to apply to the whole class to which they belong.

* The discussions of the French Conseil d'Etat on the code afford an apt view of the relation of these parts ; with regard to the former, unprofessional men could find no end ; the latter were often not spoken of at all.

Marriage belongs only half to law, half to manners: and every marriage law is unintelligible, which is not considered in connection with this its necessary supplement. Now of late, from reasons connected with the history of the christian church, the non-juridical view of this relation has become superficial, wavering and undecided in the highest degree; and this superficiality, as well as this want of certainty, have communicated themselves to the law of marriage. Whoever has carefully considered the legislation and the practical law relating to marriage, will entertain no doubt of this. Those, too, who believe that every evil requires but a remedial law for its removal, will readily admit this lamentable state, to place the necessity of a vigorous comprehensive system in a clearer light. But the hope which they here found upon legislative enactments, I hold to be altogether groundless. If, at any time, a decided and commendable tendency be distinguishable in the public mind, this may be preserved and confirmed, but it cannot be produced, by legislation; and where it is altogether wanting, every attempt that may be made to establish an exhaustive system of legislation, will but increase the existing uncertainty, and add to the difficulties of the cure.

We consider, further on, those objects which (like property) are treated with indifference by the unprofessional public, and of which even the jurists declare, that they may be the same in all circumstances,*—so that they belong exclusively to juridical technicality. Our taking this view of them is itself a proof of a state of the public mind in which the law-making faculty is deficient; for where this is alive and quick, these several relations will be any thing but indifferent; but on the contrary, will be really characteristic and necessary, as is proved by the history of every primitive system of law. Supposing this to be our condition, our capacity for legislation will depend upon the merit and cultivation of our technical law ; and our inquiries, therefore, must be next directed to this.

Unluckily, during the whole of the eighteenth century Germany was very poor in great jurists. There were numbers of laborious men, it is true, by whom very valuable preparatory labours were executed, but more than this was seldom done. A twofold spirit is indispensable to the jurist; the historical, to seize with readiness the peculiarities of every age and every form of law ; and the systematic, to

---

* Thibaut, ibid. p. 54.

view every notion and every rule in lively connection and co-operation with the whole, that is, in
the only true and natural relation. This twofold
scientific spirit is very rarely found amongst the
jurists of the eighteenth century; and, in particular,
some superficial speculations in philosophy had an
extremely unfavourable effect. A just appreciation
of the time in which one lives is very difficult:
still, unless all signs deceive, a spirit has come
upon our science, capable of elevating it for the
future to the rank of a national system. Little,
indeed, of this improvement is yet produced, and
upon this ground I deny our capacity for the production of a good code. Many may look upon this
judgment as overstrained, but I challenge them to
shew me one out of the no small number of systems
of Roman-Germanic law, which is not merely capable of being made useful in promoting this or that
particular end—for of such we have many — but
which is really good as a book. This praise, however,
can only be bestowed, when the exposition has a distinctive self-dependent form, and, at the same time,
renders the matter more vividly perceptible. Thus,
for example, in the Roman law, the point would
be to catch the method of the old jurists, the
spirit which animates the Pandects; and I should

E

rejoice to become acquainted with any one of our systems with which it were possible for this to be the case. As no work of the kind, though talents and assiduity have not been wanting, has ever yet succeeded, I maintain that, in our age, a good code is not practicable ; for with regard to this, the undertaking is the same, only more difficult. There is yet another test of our capacity : if we compare our juridical literature with the progress of German literature in general, and consider whether the first has kept pace with the latter, the result will be unfavourable, and we shall find them bearing a very different relation to each other than that borne by the Roman jurists to the literature of Rome. There is nothing degrading in this conclusion, for the task imposed upon us is really very great, — beyond comparison, more difficult than that of the Roman jurists. But we are not to mistake the magnitude of the task from indolence or self-conceit ; we are not to believe ourselves at the goal, when we are still far from it.

If then, we have really nothing which is necessary to the formation of a good code, we are not to believe that the actual undertaking would be nothing more than a disappointment, which, at the worst, would merely not have advanced us. The

great danger inevitably impending when a very
defective and shallow state of knowledge is fixed
by positive authority, has been already spoken
of; and this danger would be great in proportion
to the vastness of the undertaking and its connection with the wakening spirit of nationality. Examples, near at hand, often afford, in matters of
this kind, a less significant illustration; to make
clear, therefore, what may be the result of such a
proceeding, I will refer to the time immediately
following the decline of the Roman empire in the
West, where an imperfect state of legal knowledge
was fixed exactly in this manner. The only case
which here offers a comparison, is the Edict of
Theodoric, because in this alone the existing law
was to be stated in a new form. I am far from
believing that, what we might produce, would be
exactly like this edict; for the times are really
very different. The Romans, in the year 500,
found some difficulty in saying what they thought
—we possess some skill in composition : moreover,
there were, at that time, no juridical writers — we
have no want of these. But the similarity is not
to be mistaken in this : that there was then a mass
of historical matter to be expressed, which was not
comprehended, nor could be mastered, and which

in its new form we find some difficulty in recognising. In one respect, too, the disadvantage is on our side: in the year 500, there was nothing to spoil. In our time, on the contrary, vigorous exertions are undeniably making, and it is impossible to say how much good we subtract from the future by confirming present deficiencies. For " *ut corpora lente augescunt, cito extinguuntur ; sic ingenia studiaque oppresseris facilius quam revocaveris.*"*

An important point still remains to be considered, —the language. I ask of any one who knows what good appropriate expression is, and who does not regard language as a common tool, but as a scientific instrument, whether we possess a language in which a code could be composed ? I am far from questioning the strength of the old German language ; but that even this is not now fit for the purpose, is to me a proof the more, that we are behindhand in this circle of thought. The moment our science improves, it will be seen of how much avail our language, by its freshness and primitive vigour, will prove. What is more, I believe that, of late, we have even retrograded in this respect. I know

---

* Tacitus, Agricola, c. 3.

no German law of the eighteenth century, which, in weight and vigour of expression, could be compared with the Criminal Ordinances of Charles the Fifth.

I know what answer might be given to these reasons; even admitting all of them, it may be said, the powers of the human mind are boundless, and by reasonable exertion a work, even in these times, might be soon produced, in which none of these defects would be traceable. Well, any one may make the attempt, our age is not an inattentive one, and there is no danger that actual success will be overlooked.

I have hitherto investigated the fitness of our times for a general system of legislation, as if nothing of the kind had ever been undertaken. I now turn to the codes which recent times have actually produced.

VII.—THE THREE NEW CODES.

A COMPLETE criticism on a code, which must be of greater extent than the code itself, cannot, for that reason, be attempted within the limits of a small work. Besides, the question here does not turn so much on the particular merits of these codes, as on the prospect they hold out to us of the success or ill success of a new undertaking of the kind. All of them have originated in the same state of juridical cultivation, with reference to which our capacity for the formation of a good code has been denied; and may consequently serve, historically, as a confirmation or refutation of my argument. I take the Code Napoleon first, because on it alone detailed treatises have been published, directly applicable to my purpose.*

At the composition of this Code, the political element of legislation had a greater influence than the technical; and, for that reason, it altered the existing law more than the German codes. The causes and nature of this preponderating in-

---

* I refer to the following works : — Conférence du Code Civil avec la Discussion . . . . du Conseil d'Etat et du Tribunat. Paris, Didot, 1805, 8 vol. in 12°. Code Civil suivi de l'Exposé des Motifs (the speeches in the Corps Legislatif). Paris, Didot, 1804. 8 vol. in 12°. (Crussaire) Analyse des Observations des Tribunaux d'Appel et du Tribunal de Cassation sur le Projet de Code Civil. Paris, 1802. 4°. Maleville Analyse raisonnée de la Discussion du Code Civil, ed. 2. Paris, 1807. 4 vol. in 8°. The Code and the Project of the Code Civil are well known.

fluence have been recently so fully explained in a very talented work,† that I may here content myself with a short summary of the views contained in it.

The Revolution, then, had annihilated, together with the old constitution, a great part of the law; both, rather from a blind impulse against every thing established, and with extravagant senseless expectations of an undefined future, than in the hope of any definite improvement. As soon as Napoleon had subjected every thing to a military despotism, he greedily held fast that part of the revolution which answered his purpose and prevented the return of the ancient constitution,— the rest, which all were now sick of, and which might have proved an obstacle to himself, was to disappear ; only this was not altogether practicable, as the effects of the years that had elapsed upon the modes of thought, manners and feelings of the people, were not to be effaced. This half-return to the former state of tranquillity was certainly beneficial, and gave the Code, which was founded about this time, its principal tendency. But this return was the result of lassitude and satiety, not the victory of nobler thoughts and feelings ; nor, indeed, would there

† Rehberg on the Code Napoleon. Hanover, 1814. 8°.

have been any opening for such in that condition
of public affairs, which, to the plague of Europe,
was preparing. This want of a sound basis is discernible in the discussions of the *Conseil d'Etat,*
and must impress every attentive reader with a
feeling of despondency. To this was now added
the immediate influence of the political constitution. This, when the code was framed, was, in
in theory, republican in the revolutionary sense ;
but all, in reality, inclined to the recently developed despotism. The elements of uncertainty
and change were consequently mixed up with its
fundamental principles. Thus, for example, in
1803, Napoleon himself, in the council of state,
pronounced those same Substitutions to be injurious, of a bad moral tendency and unreasonable,
which were re-established in 1806, and, in 1807,
adopted into the code.* But as regards the state
of public feeling, a far worse consequence of this
quick succession was, that the last, so often sworn
to, object of belief and veneration was, in its turn,
annihilated, and that expressions and forms came
more and more frequently into collision with ideas,

* Conference, T. 4. p. 126. " Ces substitutions étaient contraires à l'interet de l'agriculture, aux bonnes mœurs, à la
raison, personne ne pense à les retablir."

whereby, in the greater number, even the last remains of truth and moral consistency were necessarily extinguished.

It would be difficult to imagine a state of public affairs, more unfavourable for legislation than this. Not unfrequently, even amongst the French, there glances out, in the midst of their ordinary self-commendations, a consciousness of this unhappy state, and of the imperfection of the work which emanated from it. But as regards Germany, which had escaped the curse of this revolution, the Code, (which rather carried France a part of the way backwards than a step forwards in the revolutionary path,) was consequently more pernicious and ruinous than to France herself.* All these speculations however, have fortunately only an historical interest for us Germans. Napoleon, it is true, intended otherwise. The code served him as a bond the more to fetter nations: and for that reason it would be an object of terror and abomination to us, even had it possessed all the intrinsic excellence which it wants. We are saved from

* See Rehberg, p. 141. 163. 177. 187.

† These are in substance the views of Rehberg, and I see not how they can be reproached with undue severity: the application to many particular clauses is certainly open to dispute.

this humiliation; and ere long there will remain of it little more than the recollection that so many German jurists, even without any call from without, complacently trifled with this instrument, and bade us hope for salvation from that which was meant for our destruction. At the present time, as regards Europe, the Code has assumed a different position; and we may pass a judgment upon it, calmly and impartially, considered as a code for France.

We now proceed to the technical part of the code, which might be conceived without any revolution at all, since it comprises the pre-existing law.* This pre-existing law, however, is partly Roman, partly French (*coutumes*), so that even this part of the code introduced a system of law, of which one half was new, into every particular part of France, and was welcome nowhere; † the same consequence would inevitably follow a similar attempt

* The forming a judgment on the code in this point of view was beside the purpose of Rehberg. Much excellent matter on this subject is contained in Thibaut's review of Rehberg's work in the Heidelberg Jahrb. 1814. p. 1, &c.

† Compare upon this subject the uncommonly excellent observations of the Appeal Court of Montpellier, in *Crussaire*, p. 5—9.

in Germany. Setting this consideration apart, we now turn to the work itself. Even in Germany, the earnestness and resolution with which this work was pushed on, have been frequently praised.* That the four redactors brought the principles of the whole (in the *projet de code civil*) to a conclusion in a few months, is certainly undeniable ; but all which might prove deficient in these, was to have been completed in the council of state, the pride of the French administration. That valuable reflections were often produced in these discussions, is true, but their general character has been well described by Thibaut, as " superficial, desultory, vague talking."† Still — which is here the chief point — the peculiar technicality on which the true value depended, was as good as never spoken of at all. And how could it be otherwise? Questions like the following might be made intelligible to a very numerous and mixed board : whether it should be rendered obligatory on the father to portion his daughter, and, whether a purchase might

---

* For example, Von Seidensticker's Introduction to the Code Napoleon, p. 221. 224.

† " Oberflächliches Hin-und Herreden und Durcheinandertappen." Heidelb. Jahrb. 1814. Jan. p. 12.

be impeached on the account of *læsio enormis ;* but
the general theory of the laws of things and of obligations cannot be understood at all without some
sort of scientific preparation ; nay, could not even
be mentioned in a discussion, in which the plan
was examined, article by article merely, without
examining the matter and treatment of entire
sections. It thus happened, for example, that
the discussion on the impeachment of purchases,
is at least four times as long as that upon the
two first chapters of Compacts.* Yet every man,
conversant with the subject, will concede to me,
that, as regards the general merit and utility of
the Code, those isolated questions are absolutely
insignificant compared with these universally-ap-
plicable doctrines. The *Conseil d' Etat,* therefore,
had no part in the Code, so far as it is technical ;
and the Code is and remains the very hasty work of
the known redactors,—of jurists, properly so called.
Now what was the state of jurisprudence in
France, when these jurists were formed ? It is
universally known, that, with regard to Roman law,
Pothier is the pole-star of the modern French jurists,

* That upon Art. 1674. 1685, is *Conférence,* T. 6. p. 43—94;
that upon A. 1101—1133, T. 5. p. 1—21, and the text upon it
occupies at least one half.

and that his works exercised the most immediate influence upon the code.* I am far from
undervaluing Pothier ; rather might the jurisprudence of a nation in which he was one of many, be
expected to turn out well. But a juridical literature,
in which he stands alone, and is almost revered
and studied as the source, must, notwithstanding,
be pitiable. If we more closely examine this juridical learning, as it lies in undeniable facts before us,
it is really surprising. Very significant, to go no farther, are such phenomena as Desquiron,† who talks
about a Roman jurist, one Justus Lipsius, soon after
the Twelve Tables, and of the famed Sicardus under
Theodosius the Second, framer of the Theodosian
Code † ;—monstrosities like these are alone sufficient to justify a conclusion as to the average state
of jurisprudential science. But we will turn at once
to the framers of the Code, to Bigot Preameneu,
Portalis, and Maleville. One proof of the erudition
of the first has been given already ; of Portalis,

* [Dupin, in his *Dissertation sur la vie et les ouvrages de
Pothier*, says that three fourths of the *Code Civil* were literally
extracted from his treatises. *Transl.*]

† Desquiron, Esprit des Institutes de Justinien conféré avec
le Code Napoleon. Paris, Renaudiere, 1807. 2 vol. 4°., in
the Historical Introduction.

the following may suffice : — The sixth article contains the rule, *jus publicum privatorum pactis mu-
tari non potest*. It had been objected that *jus
publicum* meant, not the law concerning the state,
but every law without distinction, every *jus publice
stabilitum*. To this Portalis replies,* that in general the word might have two meanings, but the
question is what it means in this particular part
of the Roman law. — " *Or voici comment est conçu
le sommaire de la loi* 31*me au Digeste de pactis :
contra tenorem legis privatam utilitatem continentis
pacisci licet... Ainsi le droit public est ce qui interesse
plus directement la societé que les particuliers.*" As to
this, I will not say that here *jus publicum* is su-
perficially and erroneously interpreted; but I ask
what this general rule had to do with the question, how the Romans understood a similar rule?
and, allowing it to bear some reference to the
question, how it was possible to prove the forms
of speech in use amongst the Romans from a passage of Bartolus (for the summary is his), i. e. to
class him and the Roman jurists together? This
is, indeed, *tanquam e vinculis sermocinari!* Ma-

* Moniteur an X. No. 86. p. 339. The remark forms part
of the discussions which were subsequently suppressed.

leville appears throughout his work as a respectable and intelligent man ; but particular traits of his learning are so much the more conclusive, as at the redaction of the code he was one of the representatives of the Roman law. Thus, for instance, he gives a brief sketch of the history of *Usucapio* and *res mancipi*, which is unique of its kind.* So long, says he, as the Romans had no landed property but what was small and near at hand, two years of prescription sufficed ; but when they obtained land in the provinces, consequently at a greater distance from Rome, ten years were required (the *longi temporis præscriptio*). *Res mancipi* was the term applied to landed possessions in Italy, and to all moveables ; property in moveables passed by mere delivery, and *usucapio* applied only to *res mancipi*. With regard, however, to *res nec mancipi*, i. e. to landed property in the provinces, a *longi temporis præscriptio* was allowed where there was no title: the occupant was called *dominus bonitarius*. In another place he talks about the *Usucapio* of Justinian ; we must distinguish, he says, between the thief and the third person who purchases of the thief ; the first requires thirty

* Maleville, Analyse, T. 4. p. 358. 359.

years, the other comes within the *L. un. C. de usuc. transform.*, consequently the three years' prescription,*—just as if the *res furtiva* had never been heard of amongst the Romans.

Another instance, well meriting attention, concerns Portalis and Maleville jointly. On the subject of divorce, the Roman law is constantly adduced, but Portalis and Maleville set out from a history of divorce in Rome, which is not only false, but absolutely impossible. For example, both believe that marriage could not have been dissolved by one party, but only by mutual consent (whereby, in fact, the whole law of the Pandects, nay, even the law of Justinian upon this very subject, becomes altogether senseless); that divorce by mutual consent is, amongst the Romans, but a consequence of the erroneous doctrine that marriage stands upon the same footing with other contracts ! † And this was not merely a curious question in history, but a question of principle, bearing immediately on the discussion, for the misconception of the entire history of divorce in Rome, has, to the disgust of every body, been

* Ibid. p. 407.

† Conference, T. 2. p. 123. 124. 136. The mistake of Enimery, p. 139. is a few degrees less.

adopted in Article 230. This state of juridical learning, however, is not to be regarded as pride or obstinacy; in the debates as to the rescission of sales, accident placed the Dissertation of Thomasius upon the *L. 2. C. de res vend.* in the hands of a counsellor of state, and it is really touching to see with what astonishment this work is caught up, abstracted and discussed.* We could surely supply them with similar and better erudition in other matters! Neither can this literary simplicity be laid to the charge of any national prejudice, for there were notoriously many individuals in France in the sixteenth century, from whom Roman law may still be learnt. But I myself have heard a law professor in Paris say, that the works of Cujas, it was true, could not be omitted in a complete library, but that they were no longer necessary, because all that was good in them is to be found in Pothier.

So much for the soil on which the Code has grown; now for the fruit. Completeness was not within the scope of the plan; the three following were the principal points : — Selection of subjects, — selection of rules for each subject,

* Conference, T. 6. p. 44.

F

—and relation to that which was to come in aid
(*in subsidium*) where the code should prove insufficient. The selection of subjects was, for the
practically educated jurist, the easiest; but this
has turned out so awkwardly, that, as concerns
the application, the most palpable defects are to
be found by wholesale. It was not determined
by experience and practical knowledge, but by
the impulse which the usual mode of teaching
had given; and on going farther back, it will
frequently be found, that important heads are
wanting for no other reason than because they
do not occur at all, or only incidentally, in Justinian's Institutes, which form imperceptibly the
foundation of so many new systems.* Still this
defectiveness may be regarded as a matter of indifference by us, as it would be easy to avoid it
on any future occasion.

Far more important in this respect, and much
more difficult in itself, is the selection of rules
on the subjects actually treated of; consequently, the finding of rules, by which particular
cases are to be governed in future. Here the

* Examples of important matters, wholly or in a great
measure wanting in the code, are to be found in the Heidelb.
Jahrb. 1814. Januar. p. 13.

object was to master the leading principles, on
which all certainty and efficacy in juridical matters depend, and of which the Romans afford us
so striking an example. In this point of view,
however, the French work presents a melancholy
spectacle, as is now to be shown by particular examples.

A radical defect, perceivable throughout, is the
following. The theory of the Law of Property is on
the whole Roman. The Roman Law of Property,
however, notoriously depends upon two fundamental notions — of the rights of things and of
obligations,—and every body knows how much the
Romans effected by the precision and fixedness
of these notions. Now, these are not merely no
where defined, which it was by no means my
wish to find fault with, but the redactors are
not at all acquainted with them in this extended
sense; and this ignorance spreads a greater degree of obscurity over the whole work, than could
well be believed. But this remark, important
as it is, is too general: the doctrine of the
invalidity of legal acts as applied to compacts,
to the *actes de l'état civil*, and to marriage, will
afford an opportunity of going more into particulars. With regard to the invalidity of Com-

pacts, the Roman law contains the known distinction of *ipso jure* and *per exceptionem,* which under the old law was drawn with the highest precision, and continued much more operative in the Justinian law than is commonly supposed. There is in the Code a corresponding rule upon *convention nulle de plein droit* and *action en nullité ou en rescision.* (A. 1117.) Whether the framer of this rule conceived it to be one and the same with the Roman rule, is a matter of indifference to us; but it is of great importance to observe, that the theory of this indirect invalidity (by *action en nullité*) is left wholly undefined. There is hardly any thing relating to it, except the time of prescription (A. 1304), whilst very many and very important varieties of practical operation might occur now, precisely as they occurred amongst the Romans,—consequently must be determined one way or the other, since the matter was once brought into question. For the *actes de l'état civil,* a number of forms have been prescribed, which from their nature are wholly arbitrary. (L. i. T. 2. ch. 1.) But for that very reason it was doubly necessary to fix what consequences were to follow the neglect of these forms. Some courts of justice called attention to this necessity; *

* Lyons and Rouen, *Crussaire,* p. 43. 52.

but the code contains nothing upon the subject. It might be thought that in Paris so much certainty and unanimity prevailed concerning it, that an express provision was deemed superfluous. By no means. Cambaceres assumes, that the non-observance of every form produces nullity, i. e. destroys the probatory effect of the document. Tronchet, on the other hand, says that, with regard to birth and death, there is no question at all about forms, and that falsity alone can invalidate; with regard to marriage, on the contrary, that such nullity for defect of form is certainly conceivable. * Simeon, however, assumes that the neglect of form in no case invalidates the proof, consequently, not even with regard to marriage.† If this opinion be right, all these forms were no part of the code, but merely matter of instruction to the officials; the context of the code, therefore, is directly opposed to this opinion. The matter, however, is by so much the worse, inasmuch as these forms, as far at least as the registers of deaths are concerned, are wholly impracticable in Paris, and, even in the provinces, their observance is only an object of desire. ‡

* Conférence, T. 1. p. 204. 267.
† Motifs, T. 2. p. 115.
‡ Maleville, T. 1. p. 104.

Still more important, however, is the doctrine of
the invalidity of marriage. The Roman law had here
pursued a very clear and very simple course. If
any requisite to a valid marriage was wanting, it is
declared, *non est matrimonium*, and to this non-ex-
istence any one who wished might resort at any
time. A particular suit for nullification was not
necessary, nay, not conceivable, consequently there
was not even a period of prescription, nor any other
limitation to the right. This simplicity sufficed,
because in every other case divorce at the will
of one party might be resorted to ; that it was not
resorted to in our time, was natural, and therefore,
besides this sort of nullity, (which I shall term the
Roman nullity), a particular right of invalidation
was set up, which (the name is not material) might
be termed *action en nullité*. How is this provided
for in the code ? The code supposes two sorts of
nullity, absolute and relative, (L. 1. T. 5. ch. 4.)
This might be well taken for the two opposites just
described, so that, for example, neglect of the form
of marriage would be a Roman nullity. In reality
it is so understood by Portalis,* who, with
reference to this special case, paints the true
genuine nullity in lively colours. But Maleville

* Motifs. T. 2. p. 255.

assumes the Roman nullity (the *non est matrimo-*
nium) to be independent of all these rights of invalidation (*mariage qui peut etre cassé*) and different
from it, so that, according to him, there are three
sorts : 1. *non est matrimonium* ; 2. the absolute nullity of the Code ; 3. relative nullity.* With regard
to No. 2. also, a case may well be supposed ; there
might be, for instance, a right of suit for nullification open to every one, but still a mere right of suit,
so that in default of a suit, and after the death of
one of the parties, the marriage, with all its consequences, would be valid ; only this were certainly
a superfluous subtilty. But still more confused is
the view taken by Maleville in the case of an in-
formal marriage. Such a marriage, says Art. 191,
peut etre attaqué by any one ; but Art. 193, shows
that there are cases of this kind, in which the marriage is not to be annulled, though without parti-
cularizing the cases. From both passages Maleville
draws the following conclusion :† marriage *peut être
attaqué*, i. e. a suit of nullification may be instituted ; the law forbids not the suit, but what the
judge will do is his affair ; or, in other words, the
nullification of the marriage depends on the pleasure of the judge. This, consequently, would be a

* Maleville, T. 1. p. 165. † Maleville, T. 1. p. 206.

fourth kind of invalidity, distinct from the three
before-mentioned. It is difficult to find a case in
which a discretionary power in a judge is more
dangerous and improper than in this. Whether
it really exists, I cannot say, for the law is wholly
silent upon the point, and two of the redactors, as
I have shewn, entertain directly opposite opinions
upon it. For two reasons, however, this uncertainty
is particularly injurious; first, because in Paris,
(and probably not there only) most of the poor dispense with the marriage ceremony altogether, on
account of the expence;* secondly, because the
form itself comprises a requisite of an extremely
changeable description. The ceremony must, of
necessity, take place in the presence of the *officier
du domicile* of one of the two parties, so that not
even delegation is allowed.† But the domicile
here meant is not the ordinary one (Art. 102), but
a domicile made on purpose for this ceremony,
namely, six months' residence (Art. 74); not even
a liberty of choice between the two domiciles for
this particular purpose being allowed.‡ How often,
now, in many trades, must it be a matter of doubt
whether, with the best intentions, the right officer

* Maleville, T. 1. p. 327.   † Ibid. T. 1. p. 96.
‡ Malleville, t. 1. p. 182.

has been hit upon? But in every case of the kind the whole fate of a family is left to the blind discretion of a judge, who, whatever his decision, can never be blamed for it, any decision being sure of having respectable authorities in its favour. And the first cause of this injurious uncertainty is, that people have not set out with a fixed well-defined notion, but have been wandering here and there in constant perplexity, between genuine nullity and the right of invalidation, without ever being able to emerge from the obscurity;* from which the absolute uselessness of the discussions on technical matters in the council of state, is clear. Amongst the Romans, such things were impossible, and this impossibility was not in any respect the summit of their art, but the beginning of it : that is to say, they were practical men,

* Some fruitless attempts are to be found, Conférence, T. 2. p. 79—90. The quintessence of perplexity is in the observation of Tronchet, p. 84.—Que jamais le mariage n'est nul de plein droit; il y a toujours un titre et une apparence qu'il faut détruire : When any one possesses my house, there is also *une apparence à détruire* (something merely factitious), for this the vindication is of use ; but his pretended right of property is still *nul de plein droit,* i. e. it has no existence, and I need no suit to abrogate it. With regard to testaments, it may be illustrated by the opposite rule of the old nullity on account of a son, and the *querela inofficiosi.*

whilst these redactors and councillors of state speak and write as dilettanti, or, in other words, the former did not need a code, the latter should not have been anxious to make one. Still this instance makes perfectly clear what has been said above as to the danger of unnecessary and uncalled-for legislation. A confusion of ideas, such as is here described, may exist many years, unobserved and innocuous, because the whole has been reduced by practice to a tolerable degree of consistency. Now, however, it is legislatively expressed, and, even by inconsequential discussion, is made generally known, and now it becomes dangerous, now it is a weapon in the hands of the unjust, to ensnare and overreach others. This were a political interpretation of the maxim, " *omnis definitio in jure civili periculosa est.*"

Lastly, we have still to speak, with reference to the code, of that which is to come *in subsidium,* where the code is found wanting. The French have not deceived themselves as to the extent and importance of this; they were aware, that, strictly speaking, a comparatively small number of cases could be decided directly by a text of the code; that, consequently, in almost all cases, this unrecognised something must virtually decide.*

* Portalis, in *Conférence,* T. 1. p. 29; Boulay in the Moni-

But with regard to its precise nature, they do not exactly agree ; they treat it as an undefined quantity, to which many different values may be assigned. Such, for instance, are,* 1. *équité naturelle, loi naturelle;* 2. Roman law ; 3. the old *coutumes* ; 4. *usages, exemples, décisions, jurisprudence;* 5. *droit commun;*† 6. *principes généraux, maximes, doctrine, science.* As to their widely different degrees of authority, not a word is said; except in one instance—that natural law should come *in subsidium,* if *usage* and *doctrine* should be found insufficient.‡ We shall endeavour to draw some definite conclusions from this.

In the first place, it is remarkable that one mode of supplying the deficiency, no where occurs ; namely, the organic, which from one given

teur an X. N. 86. p. 343. " *On sait que jamais, ou presque jamais, dans aucun procès, on ne peut citer un texte bien clair et bien précis de loi, en sorte que ce n'est jamais que par le bon sens et par l'equité que l'on peut décider.*"

* Conférence, T. 1. p. 27. 29. Motifs, T. 2. p. 17, 18. Maleville, T. 1. p. 13. Projet, discours preliminaire, p. xi. xii. xiii.

† Buonaparte, in Conférence, T. 2. p. 327. Avis du conseil d'état in the *Bulletin des Lois* and in *Locré,* T. 3. p. 104. " les divers cas que la loi .... a laissés a la disposition des principes généraux et du droit commun."

‡ Projet, l. c.

point (consequently from one rule of the code) deduces, with scientific certainty, another. Our jurists have some limited notions upon this subject under the names of analogy and *argumentum legis*, and even amogst the French in one instance a faint consciousness of it incidentally occurs.* But that no particular use is made of it, is probably not a matter of accident. This mode of proceeding supposes an organic unity in the code itself. But of such a unity, either material or formal, there is not even the most distant conception. Not material, for the code contains, only mechanically mixed, the results of the revolution and the pre-existing law; nay, even the pre-existing law does not cohere in the code, since it is intended to be a compromise (*transaction*) between the Roman law, and *coutumes*, as has often been boasted of it. It might constitute a formal unity, had it been reduced by the jurists, its framers, by dint of

* Projet, Discours preliminaire, p. xix. " Dans cette immensité d'objets divers, qui composent les matières civiles, et dont le jugement, dans le plus grand nombre des cas, est moins l'application d'un texte précis que la combinaison de plusieurs textes qui conduisent a la décision bien plus qu'ils ne la renferment, on ne peut pas plus se passer de jurisprudence que de lois."

hard thinking, to a logical whole, but that so high a flight was not attempted will have been made clear by the preceding representations. Nothing, therefore, it is obvious, remained, but to seek for that which was to supply the deficiency, from without.

The supplemental means before-mentioned, which are spoken of by the French authors themselves, may still be greatly reduced. Natural law is adduced more for form sake than for serious use; when particular applications are the question, no notice is taken of it, and only in Germany has the position of the French judge been deemed a subject of congratulation on account of the free use of this source of law ; * but I should like to be present when a French court decides, according to natural law, whether a marriage be invalid on account of a neglect of form in the ceremony. The remaining heads may be reduced to the two following : — 1. pre-existing law ; 2. scientific theory. These are now to be separately examined.

The pre-existing law is notoriously abrogated, not only where it comes into opposition with the code, but in all matters comprised in the Code (Art. 4), consequently, as good as totally abrogated. However, the French are more in the light as

* Schmid, Introduction to the civil law of the French empire. Vol. 1. p. 21—23. 373, 374.

to the meaning of this abrogation than the Germans, who, from antipathy or partiality to the Roman law, have disputed a good deal about it. The former take it for granted, that the judge is permitted to follow the Roman law, as well as the *coutumes,* but that he is not enjoined to do so ; that is to say, an equitable decision cannot be quashed for being contrary to this source of law.*
The same may be said of the former practice of the courts, † as we see the old *jurisprudence* cited, times out of number, as authority. Undoubtedly, it is not supposed that every judge in a case left undetermined by the code, may choose between the Roman law and any custom whatever, for this would be giving him too unlimited a power; but each is to follow the law which formerly prevailed in the vicinity, i. e. either the Roman law modified by the old practice of the courts, or some special custom with the same modifications. The necessary consequence will be, the revival of a great diversity of laws within the jurisdictions of particular appeal Courts ; and this diversity will now — when it must be established in the silence, contrary to the intention, of

---

* Maleville, T. 4. p. 414—417.

† Locré, T. 3. p. 443. ed. Paris, 1805. 8.

the code, and with confusion of ancient boun-
daries—be a real evil, which it formerly was not.
In what has been said, however, the most favourable case has been assumed—that the courts will
avail themselves, in this regular manner, of the
liberty allowed them of resorting to those remote
sources of law. But as they are under no obligation, who is answerable for it? If, therefore, in
any case that should occur, a court should adduce
any *équité* or *loi naturelle* whatever, to apply according to some peculiar opinion, or as a pretext
for an act of injustice, it cannot be made a matter
of reproach to it, for the law recognises all this
as authority. Let it not be said that the Court
of Cassation will keep the future practice in order,
or even uniform; the Court of Cassation is only
to quash in cases where any provision of the
code, or any new enactment, has been contra-
vened: consequently, a decision for or against *loi
naturelle*, Roman law, *coutume* or *jurisprudence*, is
beyond the jurisdiction of this court. Lastly,
there still remains for consideration, the important circumstance, that, in all the parts of the code
which were produced by the Revolution, the pre-
existing law affords no protection against the
blindest exertion of arbitrary power. Here, again,

the example, formerly adduced, of the invalidity of marriage may serve as an illustration.

The second possible supplement to the code, is scientific theory. On one occasion, Portalis describes this very pompously, " it is like the sea; positive laws are the shores.* In France, at present, this sea goes for very little; for a system of jurisprudence, which is not based upon sound historical knowledge, really discharges no higher duty than that of registering the practice of the courts. This is actually the case in France, and a theory, (properly speaking) distinct from the practice of the courts, does not exist there, so that all that has been said of the uncertainty of the practical law, applies also to the theory. The schools alone have, according to their nature, a purely theoretic form; these will be more conveniently spoken of in the following chapter.

Undoubtedly particular circumstances may occur, through which the state of the practical administration of justice may turn out better than is here represented. Through ignorance and supineness particular authorities and writers may be uniformly followed in many of the courts; thus, for example, the *coutume* of Paris, with its commentator, Ferriere, may be found convenient far

* Moniteur an X. p. 337.

and near, even where it had no other authority. Even under the old jurisprudence, indeed,
many rules might have been pretty generally
adopted. Probably something of the sort is intended by the before-mentioned *droit commun*.
Moreover, it must not be believed that all the
evils here mentioned would be necessarily felt
as such: the Romans of the fourth and fifth
centuries after Christ, never imagined that we
should pity them for the depth of their decline.
On the whole, however, it is undeniable, that a
state of very great uncertainty is to be apprehended. Now this state is unendurable ; whether,
indeed, different laws be in force in different places,
is of little consequence, but if, in any individual
case, the law be given up to accident and discretion, the administration of justice is reduced
to the worst conceivable condition, and the resulting mischief is sure to be universally felt.

It deserves the most honourable acknowledgment, that, in France, one honest voice at least was
heard as to what was about to be done, but this
voice died away without leaving any trace of
an effect. The Tribunal of Montpellier speaks of
the future practice of the courts, by which the
deficiencies of the code were to be supplied, as fol-

lows : " Mais quelle jurisprudence ! n'ayant d'autre règle que l'arbitraire sur l'immensité d'objets à co-ordonner au système de la legislation nouvelle, a quelle unité, à quel concert faudrait il s'attendre de la part d'une pareille jurisprudence, ouvrage de tant de juges et de tant de tribunaux, dont l'opinion ébranlée par les secousses révolutionnaires serait encore si diversement modifiée ! quelle serait enfin le régulateur de cette jurisprudence disparate, qui devrait nécessairement se composer de jugemens non sujets à cassation, puisqu'ils ne reposeraient pas sur la base fixé des lois, mais sur des principes indéterminés d'équité, sur des usages vagues, sur des idées logiciennes, et pour tout dire en un mot, sur l'arbitraire ! A un système incomplet de législation, serait donc joint pour supplément une jurisprudence défectueuse." To counteract this evil, it is said farther on, two ways may be pursued. Either consider the code merely as Institutes, and add to it a second more detailed work, which should answer the purpose of the Pandects and Code of Justinian; or, secondly and best, permit the various existing laws to remain, and only introduce new and uniform law through the whole of France in certain fixed parts; that is to say, make no code at all. This.

is the very plan of all others, and the whole method in which it is detailed and demonstrated is so
sound and purely practical, that in such com-
pany we are doubly gladdened by such original
thoughts.*

I now come to the Prussian Landrecht. As
materials for its history, the official publications
upon the subject rank first,† then, certain passages from the works of Klein; ‡ but the most
important contribution was by Simon, in 1811, on
the following occasion.§ The materials of the whole
new legislation are still in a great measure extant;

* The whole passage is reprinted in the second appendix to
this Edition.

† Cabinetsordre, v. 1780 vor dem Corpus juris Frideri-
cianum, B. 1. Berlin, 1781. 8. Die Vorerinnerungen vor
dem Entwurf des Gesetsbuchs, Th. 1. Abth. 1. and Th. 2.
Abth. 1. and 3. Cabinetsordre von 1786 in Klein's Annalen,
Th. 1. S. xlix. Publicationspatente von 1791 und 1794 vor
dem Gesetzbuch (1791), und dem Landrecht (1794).

‡ Klein's Annalen, B. 1. and B. 8, the same in the beginning of both volumes. Klein's Autobiography, Berlin, 1806.
8vo. p. 47.

§ Simon's report on the redaction of the materials of the
Prussian Legislation, in Mathis jur. Monatschrift, B. 11.
with a view of the materials. The materials for the Landrecht
alone (without the regulations of the courts) comprise from
1500 to 2000 parts in 88 folios.

to arrange and thereby fit them for use, was entrusted to the above-named jurist, and his report upon the matter gives so complete a history of the whole undertaking, that all preceding accounts appear disjointed and in part unauthentic, when compared with it. It is not possible to see in this excellent work how,—by the combined and persevering exertions of the Redactors, properly so termed, the law committee,* the provincial authorities, the deputies of the states, and many learned men and men of business from all parts of Germany, — the Landrecht was produced, without feeling the highest respect for the energy and perseverance which have been manifested in it; but the soul of the whole was the accomplished Suarez, by whom unity was given to the production of so many and such different labourers. In this point of view no unprejudiced person will compare the Code with the Landrecht; not only is the difference apparent in the good

---

* [A committee or board, composed of distinguished jurists, to whom all new laws are submitted before receiving the sanction of the royal authority. The decision of all cases of doubt relating to the interpretation of the Landrecht is also referred to them. The author is now a member of the Prussian law-committee.—TRANSL.]

faith and love for the work, which is natural to the better kind of Germans, but also in the wholly different circumstances under which the two compilations were produced. The French code was to be got ready at a moment's warning, to alleviate many pressing evils of the revolution, and to place every thing on an equal footing, whilst the Landrecht was framed with no other end or desire than that of accomplishing something excellent, without any imperative external necessity. What I regard as a second great advantage of the Landrecht, is the relation which it bears to the local sources of law. It was introduced merely as a subsidiary law in the place of " the Roman Law, the Saxon common law, and other foreign subsidiary laws and ordinances ;" * and all provincial laws were to retain their authority, but were to be reduced into particular codes within three years.† Others, on the contrary, will consider this relation as an imperfection of the Landrecht.

* Publicationspatent, s. 1.

† This, however, as regards East Prussia, took place somewhat later, (*Ostpreussisches Provincial-Recht*, Berlin 1801. 8.) As regards the other provinces, not at all. In these therefore the provincial law prevails in its old form.

If, however, we regard the composition of the Landrecht, it confirms my opinion, that no code should be undertaken at the present time. Every one knows the plan on which it was prepared. The Justinianean law was to be to such a degree the groundwork of the whole, that it was only to be departed from on particular grounds. These grounds were — when a rule of the Roman law should happen to depend on the Stoic philosophy, or the particular constitution (for example, the policy of the emperors), or upon the over-refined fictions and subtilties of the old jurists.* For this reason, the Roman law, in its relation to the Landrecht, may be divided into two parts ; one applicable, as the rule, — and one inapplicable, as the exception ; and there was a two-fold duty to be performed — to discriminate the exception properly, and to understand the rule thoroughly. But what does in fact depend on the Stoic philosophy or the particular constitution, and what is an exceptionable subtilty, can obviously be ascertained only by means of a very sound knowledge of

* Project of the Code, Part 1. Sect. 1. p. 5, 6. Klein's Annalen, B. 8. s. xxvi.—xxix. Simon, s. 197—199. Many of the most important innovations were omitted in the last revision of the Landrecht. Simon, p. 235.

legal history ; this historical knowledge, as well as the diligent study of authorities, is necessary, when the object is to understand the applicable law, and reduce it to practical application profitably. Now whether the schools of Nettelbladt and Darjes, in which most of those who exercised much influence on the Landrecht were brought up, were possessed of this historical knowledge, or had paid this attention to authorities, I leave any one to decide from the works of these schools and their masters.* The beginning of the whole was to have been a complete abstract of the law-books of Justinian. This was first proposed to Schlosser, with whom, however, it was found impracticable to agree as to the conditions.† The abstract itself, then, was made by Doctor Volkmar, after a systematic plan of Suarez; to insure its completeness, Volkmar prepared a list of all the texts of the *Corpus Juris* in the order of the authorities, remarking where each text was adopted into the system, or why it was left out. This systematic abstract was then di-

* Hugo on Daniel Nettelbladt, Civilistisches Magazin, B. 2. N. 1.

† Simon, p. 198.

gested by Volkmar and Pachaly, whose digest is to be regarded as the first material of the redaction properly so called.* This material has, on the whole, been incredibly often examined and digested, and, in fact, very little of it is left, in its original shape, in the Landrecht. But not only (generally speaking), in the execution of all extensive undertakings, does a very great deal depend upon the first impulse, but, more particularly in the present instance, much depended almost exclusively on this first ground work, and what has been done and left undone by Volkmar, must have exercised a powerful influence on all the remainder of the work. Had it been an object to avoid this influence, it would have been necessary for some one else, independently of Volkmar's work, and immediately from the authorities themselves, to work up the original materials anew, and thus alone would Volkmar's work, so far as the knowledge of, and the mode of using, the authorities are concerned, have been fairly put to the proof. This was not done; all the following revisions, to all appearance, had such an object least of

* Simon, p. 200—202.

all in view, and thus Volkmar's work* stands quite alone, although the author is treated as a mere compiler, nor appears to have been very highly esteemed. This is the very duty for which a man of talent and learning would have been most desirable; and it would be interesting, could a comparison be instituted at least in individual instances, to see how Schlosser would have executed the task. Probably, however, the nature of the arrangements made it inconvenient to assign this duty to a man of consideration and of an independent turn of mind.

On looking at the result as it lies before us, a decided opinion is more difficult than on the Code, because the discussions by which this result was produced, have not been made public. It also

---

* Simon, p. 202. There are extant the following works by Volkmar : — 1. De Condictionum indole. Hal. 1777. (Simon, p. 200.) 2. De intestatorum Atheniensium hereditatibus. Traj. ad Viad. 1778. (Schott Critik, B. 10. p. 79.) 3. Examination of the Notions of Inheritance *ex asse*, &c. Breslaw, 1780. (ib. p. 82.) 4. Varia quæ ad leges Romuleas et magistratus pertinent, Vratislav. 1779. 8°. 5. On the original Rights of Man, Breslaw, 1793. 8°. (Ersch, Literature of Jurisp. p. 272.) I am only acquainted with the fourth, and this is certainly of little importance.

appears that the plan of the work, as well as of the whole administration of law which was to be grounded upon it, was not always the same. Originally, Frederick the Second undeniably designed that the code should be in the highest degree simple, popular, and, at the same time, complete, so that the business of the judge might consist in a kind of mechanical application of the law.* Accordingly, he absolutely prohibited all interpretation, and ordered that recourse should be had to the legislative power in each particular case where the law should prove doubtful or insufficient. In the project of the Gesetzbuch, also, interpretation is forbidden to the judge, and in particular cases all is also referred to the law-committee. † Wholly otherwise according to the Landrecht; this provides that the judge shall look to the reason of the law, but

---

* Cabinetsordre of 1780, s. xii. xiii. "If I attain my object, certainly many lawyers will lose, by this simplification, their mysterious importance — be deprived of their whole retail trade in subtilties — and the whole existing corps of advocates will be rendered useless. But on the other hand I shall have more skilful merchants, manufacturers and artists, by whom the state has better hopes of profiting."

† Entwurf Einl. p. 34—36.

particularly, that he shall decide every case, for which he finds no express law, according to the general principles of the Code and the provisions for analogous cases;* the reference to the law committee was thus restricted to the greatest possible extent, and even when allowed, only the consulting judge was bound by the answer, and there were legal modes of relief against the judgment.† In the latest edition of the Landrecht, however, even this limited reference is abrogated, and the interpretation of the judge established for all descriptions of cases.‡ Thus the position of the judge is wholly different from what Frederick the Second appears to have designed, and the whole judicial office is distinguished by a more scientific and less mechanical character. Still this is but a particular deviation from the rule; it is clearly to prevail only in extraordinary cases, in which an immediately applicable law should be wanting; nay, a case of this kind, as soon as it arises, is to be pointed out and decided by a new

---

* Landrecht, Introd. s. 46—49.

† Landrecht, Introd. s. 47, 48.

‡ First appendix to the Landrecht. Berlin, 1803. s. 2.

provision.* The peculiar tendency of the existing law itself, consequently, still is, that the particular cases should be all enumerated as such, and be individually provided for. And in that respect the method of the Landrecht is in direct contrast with that, above described, which we find in the extant works of the Roman jurists; not, in my opinion, to the advantage of the Landrecht. With the Romans, all depends on the jurist, by his thorough mastery of the system, being placed in a condition to find the law for every case that may arise. This is effected by the precise individual perception of particular legal relations, as well as by the thorough knowledge of the leading principles, their connection and subordination; and where, with them, we find law cases in the most restricted application, they notwithstanding constantly serve as the embodied expression of the general principle. That this difference exists, will be allowed by every one, who, without prejudice, compares the Landrecht with the Pandects, and such a comparison is certainly allowable here, since we are obviously not discussing the peculiar constitution of Rome, but the universal method. As to what, in particular,

* Landrecht, Introd. s. 50.

concerns the precise definite comprehension of the
notions, the not unfrequent want of it in the Landrecht is the less perceptible, because even the material completeness of the detail tends in its way to
supply these deficiences. But with regard to the
practical rules, which form the proper object of
every code, the consequence of the character here
described is, that most of the provisions of the
Landrecht neither reach the height of universal
leading principles, nor the distinctness of individuality, but hang wavering between the two, whilst
the Romans possess both in their natural connection.
However, it must not be overlooked that a great, perhaps insurmountable, difficulty presented itself in
the present state of the German language, which,
generally speaking, is not juridically formed, and
least of all for legislation : to what extent the vivid
exposition of individual legal relations is thus rendered difficult, nay impossible, may be discovered
by any one who will make but one trial of
the kind,—for instance, a translation from the
Pandects. In this respect, it must be owned, the
French had a great advantage over us in the
greater fixedness of their forms, and in the Latin
derivation of their language : that they have not
made better use of it, is accounted for by the low

state of knowledge above described amongst them.
These observations would be very much misunderstood, were they understood to intimate that the
framers of the Landrecht were indifferent as to the
future scientific study of it, which is by no means
my opinion. On this point, the well-known prize
question of 1788 * merits consideration; which required a manual in two parts, of which the first was
to contain a law of nature abstracted from the Code,
the second, an abstract of the positive law itself.
This notion of the law of nature was very supercili-
ously received, and thereby injustice was done to it:
certainly, under this name, that ought to have been
set forth, which the legislator himself regards as
universal, and not of mere positive enactment, in
his laws,—an interesting historical problem, exactly
resembling that of the Roman *jus gentium*. Thus
the scientific knowledge of the practical law was
by no means made light of; on the contrary, the
Landrecht, in its latest form, recognises the imperative necessity for this scientific knowledge.
However, it is clear that this acknowledgment is
at variance with the context of the work itself;
since this context leans towards the original idea

* Entwurf, Th. 2. Abth. 3.   Vorerrinnerung.

of Frederick the Second, from which, indeed, it emanated.

Every government is to blame which is ignorant of, or disregards, the intelligence of its age. In this respect, however, the Prussian legislation is certainly not open to reproach. The voices, not merely of professional men, but of all the learned of Germany,* were invoked and listened to ; and every unprejudiced observer will allow that what has been done, as well as what has been left undone, is in perfect harmony with the feeling and spirit of the age. Even the most important voice which was raised on the other side at the time,† proves more for, than against, this opinion. I am not ignorant how much excellence is contained in the views and opinions of Schlosser, but what is best in them relates to the general political character of our times, and what he says relating to the peculiar wants of the law, is by no means unobjectionable. This appears partly from his Introduction to a code, ‡ and, still more

---

* In Simon, p. 213, 220, are the names of those who sent in remarks, or obtained prizes.

† Schlosser's Briefe über die Gesetzgebung &c. Frankfurt, 1789, und Fünfter Brief, &c. Frankfurt, 1790. 8º.

‡ Briefe, p. 246.

from his plan for reducing the *corpus juris* to a *caput mortuum* of enactments of less than ten books.* That he was not deficient in the true juridical spirit is evident from his talented and throughout excellent article upon the study of the pure Roman law. †

A complete judgment on the technicality of the Landrecht would only be practicable, should the materials already enumerated be digested and made universally known. All that has been done for the preservation and diffusion of important historical authorities, deserves honourable acknowledgment; so does the organization of those materials, which was planned and then executed in the most admirable manner by the chief of the Prussian lawyers, the minister of justice, Von Kircheisen. But still it is to be hoped that the same liberal interest in the internal history of the Landrecht, will also lead to the publication of a good abstract of it. There is nothing to be afraid of in such undertaking, for what has

* Schlosser's Vorschlag und Versuch einer Verbesserung des Deutschen Bürgerlichen Rechts, &c. Leipzig, 1777. 8º. Schlosser's Letters, p. 46. 342, where he praises the writings of Westphal as very useful for this purpose.

† In Hugo's Civilist. Magazin, B. 1. n. 6. (1790.)

been so deliberately executed may quietly abide any judgment whatever. That in this manner, even in the above mode of viewing the whole, many a particular may be found to be untenable, is true ; but this would clearly be a very fortunate result, for such a means of purifying itself is desirable in every system. These materials cannot fail to be more instructive than what have been printed relating to the code, for the latter refer almost exclusively to the transition from the *projet* to the code. With regard to the formation of the *projet* itself, which is by far the more important matter, they afford no explanation ; unless the empty declamations of the greater number of the discussions may pass current for such. Those materials, on the contrary, would carry us back even to the first conception of the plan. There would be, however, one particular advantage : the Landrecht would thus gain an historical and scientific existence, which up to the present time has been altogether wanting to it. At the same time, it by no means follows that it will suffer any injustice from unfair adversaries ; for amongst the clever and highly educated men, of the number of which the Prussian ministry of justice may well be proud, several would certainly be found capable of defending it from any injustice of the sort.

The history of the Austrian Gesetzbuch * is so far similar to that of the Prussian Landrecht, that each received its first impulse about the middle of the last century,† so that the very same state of German juridical literature could operate on each. The groundwork was a manuscript work of eight large folios, mostly extracted from the commentators on the Roman law, and completed as early as 1767. Horten made an abstract of this, which was digested into a code by Martini. This work of Martini was then published ; and examined and decided upon by the Austrian provincial authorities and Universities,‡ from which revised copy the present Gesetzbuch was finally framed. The co-operation of the jurisconsults of the rest of Germany appears to have been very insignificant ; indeed, their assistance does not appear to have been thought particularly desirable, partly on account of the bad success of a prize-question upon usury ; partly because the Prussian Landrecht had already

* The information relating to it is taken from Zeiller's Vorbereitungen zur neuesten Oesterreichischen Gesetzkunde. Wien. und Triest, 1810. B. 1. p. 19—30.

† Of the Prussian, in 1746 ; of the Austrian, in 1753 Simon, p. 194. Zeiller, p. 19.

‡ Zeiller, p. 23. 26—30.

115

received contributions of the kind, which consequently were equally available for the Gesetzbuch: for this reason prizes were not publicly offered as in Prussia. There might be good reasons for not offering prizes, but, even without prizes, suggestions and opinions might have been easily procured; only, considering the very limited literary intercourse of the rest of Germany with Austria, the mere printing of the *projet* was certainly not enough; a circular to all the German universities would hardly have been unsuccessful. Thus this undertaking, which, from its nature, ought to have been based on nothing less than the science of the whole nation, has been completed like an ordinary transaction of the particular country; and every separation of this kind is fraught with danger to, if not altogether decisive against, the result.

As for the contents — from the directions of the Empress Maria Theresa, a greater degree of originality might have been expected than in the Prussian system, since the framer was not to confine himself to the Roman law, but was to allow natural equity to be of force throughout.* But what has been said of the formation of the first ground-work

* Zeiller, p. 24.

H 2

from the commentators, as well as the consideration of the Gesetzbuch itself, shews that the same
sources, only less pure and immediate, were resorted to as in the case of the Landrecht. In
the composition, a main distinction is instantly
discoverable ; viz. that, in the Gesetzbuch, no
attempt has been made, as in the Landrecht, to
provide directly for all the cases that may arise,
but only to define the notions of legal relations, and
lay down the most general rules for them.* In
the whole form and design, the work closely
resembles a somewhat detailed compendium of institutes. The execution is now to be subjected to
a more careful examination, partly with reference
to the notions (the formal or theoretic part),
partly with reference to the practical rules.

That the notions of legal relations, in a work on
this plan and of this extent, must be of paramount
importance, is self-evident. In the Prussian Landrecht, they are of less consequence, by reason
of its richness in practical rules ; and the faulty
mode of treating them is less injurious. And
precisely in this respect there is much to object
against the Gesetzbuch. The notions of rights,

* The three parts of the Gesetzbuch contain together 561
widely printed pages.

are too general and undefined, and too much grounded on the mere letter of the Roman law, or even on the misconceptions of recent commentators on that law, which would not have been possible, had the authorities been thoroughly understood. The Gesetzbuch has both these defects, not only in common with the Landrecht, (which, as above observed, is less affected by them), but even in a greater degree, as is now to be shewn by particular examples. The question here, however, is as to the construction of the notions themselves, not of definitions; to which, as mere symptoms of that construction, only a conditional and subordinate value can be ascribed, and which, only in this relation and not for their own sakes, will be the subject of the following considerations. In the first place, it has been already observed in speaking of the code, how important and generally applicable the very precise notions of the law of things are in the Roman law. The same holds good of the notion of *Status*. Here, now, lies the fundamental distinction between the laws of persons, and the laws of things, (s. 14, 15.) which, however, are not considered as fixed in either the Roman or in any other way. The Landrecht (I. 2. s. 122—130.) is more

accurate upon the point. The notion of *thing*
(s. 285. compare s. 303.) is so generally defined,
that there is hardly any thing which may not be
termed *thing :* arts, learning, skill, ideas, are included in *thing*, in this general sense. Now, two of
the most important law-notions are directly grounded upon the notion of *thing : possession*, (s. 309.) and
property (s. 353, 354.) But it is clear that, for
this very reason, these notions are unformed and
useless throughout; thus, for example, according
to s. 309, we must ascribe to a man of learning the
legal possession of his learning, for he has it in his
power, and has the will to keep it. In treating of this
doctrine, therefore, a narrower, undefined notion of
thing has imperceptibly crept in; but even this
tacitly introduced notion is not sufficient, for, according to it, there must still be possession and
property in an obligation, which by a loose mode
of speech may certainly be said, but which is nevertheless at variance with the whole theory of Possession and Property. The Landrecht (I. 2. s. 3.)
affords some assistance here by a distinctly expressed, more limited notion of *thing*, to which the legal
relations are subsequently referred. A still more
general disadvantage of that useless notion of
thing, appears at once in the division of the

rights of things into real and personal, (s. 307.)
Under the head of *real*; the well-known five
kinds are enumerated — Possession, Property,
Pledge, Servitude, and Inheritance (s. 308.); the
mere collocation of which is sufficient to render
any definite generic notion impossible. The objects
of Prescription are so generally laid down, (s. 14.
55.) that many rights might be classed under it,
to which, however, this mode of acquisition could
only be applied by a very forced and very superfluous construction, — an application which probably
was never intended. The Landrecht (I. 9.) pre-
cludes this doubt, by treating the whole doctrine
under the head of Modes of acquiring Property.
Under the head of Personal Servitudes, the right
of use, and that of usufruct, are distinguished
as follows : that the former is to be limited to
the mere wants of the occupant, the latter not,
(s. 504. 509.) The practical sense of this is, that
compacts and wills, when they speak of a right
of use, are to be understood to mean a right of
use of the limited kind. But this construction is
certainly not natural, since it is by no means customary to express such a right by the term *use*.
How this notion originated, cannot be a subject of doubt ; it is the *usus*, in opposition to

the *usufructus*; not, however, the very *usus* of the Roman jurists, but that which has been erroneously adopted in our compendia, down to the most recent times. The Romans understood by *usus*, the use without the *usufruct*; for example, in the case of a horse, the riding and driving, but not the offspring and the hire. It is only when, from inadvertence, the *usus* of a thing is given, of which this pure use is wholly or partly impracticable, that, departing from the ordinary course, they interpret *usus* to mean complete or partial *usufructus*; taking it for granted, as a necessary consequence, that an incorrect expression has been used, for which reason interpretation may be resorted to. The peculiar existence of this *usus* depends upon the Roman idiom, and as we have no word of corresponding preciseness, the Landrecht adopted the proper course — to take no notice of *usus*, and, without reference to *usufruct*, to declare first, in general terms, that the limited rights of use may be conferred at will, (I. 21. s. 227.) and then treat of such cases of the kind as are yet common amongst us.

The difference between guardian and curator (s. 188.) might, at the first view be placed in this — that the former would relate to minors, the latter to all others who might stand in need of protection. This terminology would certainly be new and peculiar to the Gesetzbuch, and yet unobjectionable. But it is not so; for even minors often have a curator, and not a guardian, (s. 270—272.) This is undoubtedly borrowed from the Roman law, which also, it is well known, frequently gives the ward a mere curator; except that, in that law, all minors have been properly classed with wards. But there is a particular reason for this marked distinction between tutelage and curatorship in the Roman law. The tutor, in the Roman law, is the person by whose authority the incapacity of the ward, otherwise incapable of acting, may be supplied, whilst every *curator* is no other than the ordinary administrator of the rights of others. The distinctive and important function of the Roman tutor therefore is, that through him, mancipations, stipulations, vindications, &c. are in the power of the ward; which transactions could not be undertaken at all by a mere representative, not, consequently, by a curator. Thus, the key of the whole institution of tutelage, in so far as it was peculiar and different from curatorship, lay in the rule — *per extraneam personam nihil adquiri (neque alienari) potest ;* this rule was, it is true, at a later period, limited to civil transactions ;† but with regard to these it was still in force in Justinian's time, as is proved by the passages cited from his books of law. We, on the contrary, in our practical laws, have no longer any trace of it, and, consequently, no reason for retaining the Roman distinction between tutor and curator, which has lost its meaning for us. The Gesetzbuch endeavours, at the very first mention of guardian, (s. 188.) to exclude the cases, in which the trustee of a minor is merely a curator; this is done by the definition : " A guardian is, more particularly, to take care of the person of the minor; but at the same time, to manage his property." In its particular relation to the person, therefore (although, according to s. 282, the same relation may occur in the case of curators), lay the distinctive peculiarity of guardianship. This, undoubtedly, is now the rule of the Roman law: personæ, non rei vel causæ (tutor) datur ;‡ which has been modified in our new compendia in exactly the same way as in the Gesetzbuch, because

---

* S. 5. 1. per quas pers.

† S. 1. cit. L. 53 D. de adqu. rer. dom.

‡ L. 14. D. de testam. tut.

it was not to be concealed that the tutor has clearly something to do with the property. * With perfect consistency, therefore, the right and the duty of education are devolved upon the guardian as fully as on the father (s. 216.); in matters relating to which he is only bound to obtain the approval of the court in important and critical emergencies.

But the meaning of that rule of the Roman law is wholly different; the *persona* of which it speaks, is the legal personal capacity of the ward, his capacity for formal transactions. To render this capacity complete (is meant by the passage) is the principal duty of the tutor; for that reason, his function must extend over the whole property, and cannot be limited to particular legal relations of the ward. For that reason, again, the Roman tutor has nothing at all to do with the education of the ward ; this being provided for by the prætor, acting discretionally according to circumstances, who is at liberty to choose the tutor as well as any other person.† It may be objected, that, upon good grounds, it has been

---

* Hellfield, s. 1298. " Ipsa vero tutela consistit in defensione personæ pupilli principaliter, et secundario in defensione bonorum pupillarium."

† Digest. lib. 27. tit. 2.

thought desirable to alter this very provision of the Roman law. Well and good ; but, at the same time, the remaining connection presents no trifling difficulty. For the Gesetzbuch has adopted, from the Roman law, the strict right of the nearest relatives to the *tutela legitima*, (s. 198.) and this general power of the heir *ab intestato** over the person of the minor, is of a very critical description. We need not take the extreme case of the guardian's murdering the ward in order to inherit from him : in many other cases that have escaped observation, the interest of the ward, so far as the care of his person and education are concerned, will be very different from that of his presumptive heir. Against these no protection is afforded, either by the legal grounds of incapacity for guardianship, (s. 191. 193.) which will very seldom be of a nature to be specified ; or by the superintendance of the court, which, indeed, is only required to be resorted to in critical emergencies, (s. 216.) ; or, lastly, by the proofs which may subsequently be produced of

---

* By the Roman law the heir *ab intestato* was, in all cases, expressly called to the guardianship. By the Austrian Gesetzbuch, it is possible for the heir *ab intestato* and the nearest relative entitled to the guardianship, to be different persons ; but in most cases, even in this system, the person will be one and the same.

the actual abuse of the power, (s. 217.) In this case, the organic connection of various rules of law is well worthy of observation. The Roman law renders it's *tutela legitima* innoxious, by separating the education from it; the principal duty of the tutor is, to empower; and, certainly, of no man is it to be feared less than of the future heir, that he will assent to inconsiderate alienations or obligations. By the Prussian Landrecht, as by the Roman law, the court has the direct appointment of the person to whom the minor's education is confided, without being tied down to the guardian, (II. 18. s. 320.); and no particular relative has any right to the *tutela legitima,* independently of the appointment of the court, (II. 18. s. 199.); which exactly agrees with our present view of guardianship. In defining the notion of guardianship, also, the Landrecht goes more freely to work : in it, the guardian is he who has to provide for all, the curator only for particular, occasions, (II. 18. s. 3. 4.) On this subject, the Roman terminology is very properly disregarded ; but its place is supplied by the context. Thus, for example, even the idiot has now a guardian, (II. 18. s. 12.) who, by the Austrian Gesetzbuch, has only a curator, (s. 270.) The latter follows, in this respect, the Roman law ;

but the reason, in the Roman law, for accurately distinguishing the guardianship of the pupil from that of the idiot, was, that, in the case of the pupil, but not in that of the idiot, an *auctoritas* was possible; which reason no longer exists. That things of this kind are trifling and insignificant, no one will maintain, who has attentively considered the great influence of this connection and exposition of notions upon the rules of law themselves.

Hitherto we have been speaking of the formation of the notions in the Gesetzbuch, and only incidentally of the practical rules, — that is, so far only as these were immediately influenced by such formation. We have now, however, to speak particularly of these practical rules. It has been already observed, that the completeness, aimed at in the Landrecht, was not even attempted in the Gesetzbuch. It will be, therefore, with the Gesetzbuch as with the Code; it will generally be found impossible to decide particular cases directly by means of it; and that which lies without it, by which they will be actually decided, here also merits the greatest possible attention. The Gesetzbuch itself (s. 7.) prescribes two sources of this sort of supplement: the provisions for analogous cases actually contained in the code, and, where these prove insufficient, natural law. But the first is little to be depended upon ; for material fulness as already observed, was not the object in the composition of the Gesetsbuch, and its formal insufficiency has been discussed in detail. The second source, however, (natural law) has been admitted by those worthy men themselves, who last assisted in the compilation of the Gesetsbuch, to be fraught with danger to the administration of justice.* The result consequently, with the Gesetsbuch as with the code, will be wholly different from what appears to have been anticipated ; inasmuch as scientific theory will inevitably and imperceptibly exercise that very influence upon the administration of justice, which the Gesetsbuch was framed to withdraw from it. In reality, therefore, most will depend upon the question whether this actually-operating and widely-spread theory be good or bad ; and the

---

* Zeiller. ibid. p. 38. " As, however, every man in matters of philosophy now decides according to his own conviction ; just so it is easy to conceive that the decisions are often pronounced according to a fanciful equity (æquitas cerebrina) and in reality according to arbitrary will."

condition of the law-schools (to be treated of in the following chapter) will be decisive of the administration of justice, with reference to considerations wholly different from those involving the mere knowledge of the Gesetzbuch itself.

If this judgment upon the three new codes be well founded, it forms a confirmation of my argument, that the present time has no aptitude for the undertaking of a code; and a very strong confirmation indeed. How much the French are able to perform by means of their readiness and facility in practical life, has often enough been repeated to us all; we know, moreover, for how long a period meritorious intelligent men were zealously employed upon the German codes. If then, notwithstanding such multiform exertions, the end has not been attained, there must be some insurmountable obstacles in the juridical state of the whole age. This consideration, however, is decisive, as undoubtedly the zealous partizans of codes find no security for a successful result, except in their own persevering exertions, which those experiments prove to be inadequate. Nothing remains, therefore, but to compare the present state of jurisprudence

with that from which the existing codes emanated,
and, on an unprejudiced self-examination, we must
own, that, although they may possibly differ in degree, they do not differ in kind.

These several observations, I should add, do not
at all apply to particular imperfections, by the removal of which a really excellent and sufficient
whole could be produced, but, on the contrary, to
the character of the whole itself, and every particular that has been cited, was only cited to illustrate this general character, and support an opinion
of that. A recent writer* is of a different opinion:
he believes that the few spots to be found upon the
code might easily be wiped away, when it would
become a blessing richly meriting our gratitude.
But, according to him, this foreign wisdom is
superfluous to us; "for," says he, "we have within
a short period established a code in Austria, which
may at least be placed alongside of the French
code, and which has, for us, the additional advantage of being applicable to all Germany, without further preparation." His advice is, that this
code be immediately adopted, and that it be then
left to the governments to submit their proposals

* K. E. Schmid, Deutschlands Wiedergeburt, p. 131. 134,
135.

I

for particular alterations to a legislative committee. This opinion may, it appears to me, be refuted without examining the real merits of these two codes; for were it true that the French code is excellent, and would be, with some slight modifications, a blessing, — that the widely different Gesetzbuch is also excellent, nay, still better, and exactly adapted to us ; — an excellence of a purely mechanical character must be ascribed to codes, and it would be impossible to regard them as any thing grand and highly desirable.

VIII.—WHAT WE ARE TO DO WHERE THERE ARE NO CODES.

In considering the course to be pursued, we must distinguish between those countries in which common-law and provincial-law (only somewhat interrupted by the brief reign of the code) were in force up to the present time, from those which are already living under codes of domestic manufacture.

In the countries where the common law prevails, as in all others, a good state of the law will depend on three things; first, sufficient authorities; secondly, a sufficient ministry of justice; lastly, good forms of procedure. I shall subsequently refer to these three points, as tests of the soundness of my plan.

With regard, in the first place, to the authorities, to which even the proposed code was to conform, the same mixed system of common-law and provincial-law, which formerly prevailed throughout the whole of Germany, ought, in my opinion, to be substituted for the code, or retained where the code was not in force: I hold these authorities to be sufficient, nay, excellent, provided jurisprudence does what it ought to do, and what can only be done by means of it. For if we consider our actual condition, we find ourselves in the midst of an immense mass of juridical notions and theories which have descended, and been multiplied, from generation to generation.* At present, we do not possess and master this matter, but are controlled and mastered by it, whether we will or not. This is the ground of all the complaints of the present state of our law, which I admit to be well-founded: this, also, is the sole cause of the demand for codes. This matter encompasses and hems us in on all sides, often

* Rehberg on the Code Napoleon, p. 8—10.

without our knowing it. People might think to annihilate it, by severing all historical associations,
and beginning an entirely new life. But such an
undertaking would be built on a delusion. For it
is impossible to annihilate the impressions and
modes of thought of the jurists now living, — impossible to change completely the nature of existing
legal relations; and on this twofold impossibility
rests the indissoluble organic connection of generations and ages; between which, development only,
not absolute end and absolute beginning, is conceivable. In particular, the altering of single, nay
of many, legal doctrines, is doing absolutely nothing towards this object; for, as before observed,
the modes of thought, with the speculations and
questions that may arise, will still be influenced
by the pre-existing system, and the subserviency
of the past to the present will manifest itself
even where the present is purposely opposed to
the past. There is consequently no mode of avoiding this overruling influence of the existing matter ; it will be injurious to us so long as we igno-
rantly submit to it ; but beneficial, if we oppose to
it a vivid creative energy,—obtain the mastery over
it by a thorough grounding in history, and thus appropriate to ourselves the whole intellectual wealth

of preceding generations. We have, therefore, no choice but either, as Bacon says, *sermocinari tamquam e vinculis,* or to learn by the profound study of jurisprudence, how to use this historical matter freely as our instrument: there is no other alternative. Were we to adopt the last, the scientific principle, as the nobler part, might of itself gain on its own account: our present position, too, affords particular grounds for this opinion. First, the general turn for science, which is natural to the Germans, and whereby they have been enabled to take the lead of other nations in many things; secondly, much in our political circumstances. For this reason, the experience of other nations or times cannot be adduced in opposition; neither the state of the law in England, nor the state of the law in the time of our forefathers. As to our forefathers, Möser has explained in an excellent article,* the difference between what he calls arbitrariness and what he calls wisdom; with the former, freedom and justice might consist, so long as juries formed of the peers of the parties adjudicated; we can never dispense with wisdom. As a substitute for it, the adherence to middling authorities deserves in this respect (bad as it may be in others) all

* On the mode in which our forefathers have abridged lawsuits.—*Patriotic Fancies,* Th. 1. N. 51.

estimation,* and may serve as a means of protection against the ruinous alternation of arbitrariness and wisdom.

Only when by zealous study we shall have perfected our knowledge, and, more particularly, sharpened our historical and political sense, will a sound judgment on the matter that has come down to us be possible. Until then it might be more prudent to pause before considering the existing law as loose practice, impolitic exclusiveness, and mere juridical apathy :† but, most especially, to hesitate upon the application of the dissecting knife to our present system. In applying it we might strike unawares upon sound flesh, and thus charge ourselves with the heaviest of all responsibilities to posterity. The historical spirit, too, is the only protection against a species of self-delusion, which is ever and anon reviving in particular men, as well as in whole nations and ages; namely, the holding that which is peculiar to ourselves to be common to human nature in general. Thus, in times past, by the omission of certain prominent peculiarities, a natural law was formed out of the Institutes, which

---

* Möser's Schreiben eines alten Rechtgelehrten über das sogenannte allegiren, a. a. O th. 1. N. 22.

† Thibaut, p. 52, 55, 60.

was looked upon as the immediate emanation of reason. There is no one now who would not regard this proceeding with pity ; and yet we meet with people daily, who hold their juridical notions and opinions to be the offspring of pure reason, for no earthly reason but because they are ignorant of their origin. When we lose sight of our individual connection with the great entirety of the world and its history, we necessarily see our thoughts in a false light of universality and originality. There is only the historical sense to protect us against this, to turn which upon ourselves is indeed the most difficult of applications.

One might be tempted to admit this historical grounding of the matter in which we are necessarily involved, to be necessary in our present position, but, at the same time, to consider it an evil, from its engrossing energies which might be directed to more useful ends. This would be a melancholy view, because the feeling of an inevitable evil would be excited by it ; but we may console ourselves with the conviction that it is false. On the contrary, this necessity is to be deemed a great good in itself. In the history of all considerable nations we find a transition from circumscribed, but fresh and

vigorous, individuality, to undefined universality.
The law undergoes the same, and in it, likewise,
the consciousness of nationality may, in the end,
be lost. Thus it happens, that, when old nations
reflect how many peculiarities of their law have already dropped off, they easily fall into the error
just mentioned, holding all the residue of their law
to be a *jus quod naturalis ratio apud omnes homines
constituit.* That, at the same time, the peculiar
advantage, by which the old law was characterised,
is lost, is obvious. To talk of going back to this
past time, were a vain and idle proposition ; but it
is a wholly different affair to keep its distinguishing
excellencies fully in view, and thus guard our minds
against the narrowing influence of the present,—
which is certainly both practicable and salutary.
History, even in the infancy of a people, is ever
a noble instructress, but in ages such as ours she
has yet another and holier duty to perform. For only
through her can a lively connection with the primitive state of the people be kept up ; and the
loss of this connection must take away from
every people the best part of its spiritual life.
That, consequently, by which according to this
theory, the common law and the provincial laws
are to become truly useful and unobjectionable as

authorities, is the strict historical method of jurisprudence. Its character does not consist, as some recent opponents have strangely maintained, in an exclusive admiration of the Roman law ; nor in desiring the unqualified preservation of any one established system, to which, indeed, it is directly opposed, as has been shown by the above judgment on the Austrian Code. On the contrary, its object is to trace every established system to its root, and thus discover an organic principle, whereby that which still has life, may be separated from that which is lifeless and only belongs to history. But the subject matter of jurisprudence, which is to be treated in this manner, is, with regard to the common law, threefold, from which three principal divisions of our jurisprudence are derived : Roman law, German law, and new modifications of the two. The Roman law (as already observed) besides its historical importance, has the advantage of being able, by reason of its high state of cultivation, to serve as a pattern and model for our scientific labours. This advantage is wanting to the Germanic law ; but this law possesses another not inferior advantage. It is directly and popularly connected with us, and we are not to allow ourselves to be led astray by the circumstance that most of the primitive forms have, to all practical purposes, disappeared. For the national foundation of these forms, the turn of mind from which they emanated, outlives the forms themselves, and it is not to be decided beforehand, how much of the old Germanic institutions, political as well as legal, may be revived. * Not indeed in letter, but in spirit; though it is only from the old letter that we learn to become acquainted with the original spirit. Lastly, the modification of the two primitive systems is not to be slighted. For during the long course, reaching to our time, which these primitive systems have run, much of a wholly different character has naturally established and developed itself; partly to meet the actual wants of the people as they arose, partly, in a more scientific manner, in the hands of the jurists. This last preponderates here, and the history of our jurisprudence from the middle ages downwards, forms its groundwork. One principal object of this third division of our science ought to be the gradual

* [From an article by M. Warnkoenig, (Thémis, tom. 10.) it appears that the study of German law is rapidly advancing. MM. Eichhorn and Mittermaier are particularized as the most eminent of its cultivators; and honourable mention is also made of MM. Hüllmann, Maurer, Gaupp, Albrecht, Homeyer, and George Phillips.—TRANSL.]

purification of the present system from that which
has been produced through the mere ignorance
and dullness of uncultivated times, without any
real practical demand for it.

It is not my intention to describe, methodically
and in detail, this historical mode of treating all the
parts of our law ; but something must be added as
to the Roman law, its treatment having recently
been made a subject of discussion. What I hold
to be the only possible basis of this branch of
study, will appear from my former remarks on
the Roman law. It is the law of the Pandects,
by which the transitions to the new modifications down to Justinian, are then to be fixed.
No one will deem this opinion capricious, who
considers that it was entertained by Justinian,
and that, nominally at least, it has been for
ages the basis of the principal courses of instruction at the universities, and of the most co-
pious works on the Roman law. It is not difficult to say how the old jurists are to be studied,
though difficult to make it obvious without actual trial ; they are not merely to remain a dead
letter in the schools, but to be regenerated ; we are to
read and think in their spirit, as in that of any other
authors whom we thoroughly appreciate ; we are to

familiarize ourselves with their modes of thought, and be so thoroughly imbued with them, as to compose in their style, and on their principles, and thus continue, in its true spirit, the work they were prevented from consummating. That this is possible, is one of my liveliest convictions. The first requisite is certainly a sound knowledge of legal history, and (which necessarily results from it) the confirmed habit of viewing every notion and every doctrine in its proper historical light. There is still much to be done in this department; but whoever considers what our legal history was five-and-twenty years ago, and how very different a thing it has become (as respects the more diffused knowledge of it, and the mode of treating it), chiefly through the meritorious exertions of Hugo, may surely entertain the best hopes of the result. He who has made himself thoroughly at home with the sources of the Roman law in this manner, will, it is true, still find the study of our more recent juridical literature, from the middle ages downwards, a labour, and often a repulsive labour; but thus only can he mature his opinions and rectify his views,—consequently, find no intrinsic difficulty therein. He, on the other hand, who does not thus grapple with the Roman law at the root, will, by that modern literature, be almost inevitably involved deeper and deeper in vacillation and uncertainty; unless he make up his mind to remain ignorant of the whole, and leave it to chance to determine what individual, recent, probably very shallow, summary of this literary development he is to be formed by ; a course of proceeding very frequently adopted in modern times. The literary filling-up here indicated, however, is a step in the gradual perfecting, not a part of the necessary foundation, of the study. The foundation must certainly be laid in the lectures of the universities, and for that purpose a year and a half or two years (which, as is well known, it has hitherto been customary to devote to it) might be sufficient.—Not sufficient to form a finished jurist, which indeed no reasonable man will expect from any course of university study whatever; but quite sufficient to be at home in the original authorities, to learn to read them without assistance, to read and form his own opinion of modern writers, and not to be led astray by them. It is clear that the experience of an actual course of study cannot be appealed to on the other side, provided the immediate introduction to the original authorities has not been attempted in such course.

Two opinions have been recently pronounced, differing from this theory and diametrically opposed to each other, as to the requisites of legal study amongst us. Thibaut,* for one, represents the difficulty of it as almost terrific, and in a manner that cannot fail to daunt the courage of every one who might wish to follow it; thus, for example, according to him, we may probably be lucky enough at the end of a thousand years, and not before, to have works, exhaustive of the subject, on all the doctrines of the Roman law. This is too little or too much, as it is taken. An important historical problem is never so exhausted or settled, as that no farther progress is possible,— not even in a thousand years; but we do not need so long a time to gain a surer view of the Roman law, and a chance of a more immediate and judicious application of it. This is even now practicable to a great degree, although the law itself is constantly progressing, which I do not consider blameable in our science, but highly honourable to it. All depends upon the mode in which the study is pursued. A hundred years ago, far more time and trouble were devoted to the Roman law in Germany than now; and it is undeniable that

* Ibid. p. 15—22.

no such progress in the proper knowledge of it could be made as is now practicable with good teachers. Moreover, there is no great reason to be afraid of critical difficulties, which Thibaut speaks of as insurmountable.* He who sets about it properly, may easily, with a very imperfect edition of the Pandects, master the method of the Roman jurists: many particular errors he would certainly fall into, but with the help of three or four editions such as any man may easily procure, and a little critical skill, he will be in a condition to correct even these with certainty. Here, also, two distinct things are wholly confounded; that, namely, which is essential to the gradual and exhaustive development of a great historical problem, with that which is the indispensable requisite of a direct, practical, in a certain sense satisfactory, degree of sound knowledge. Every thing which Thibaut here says of the uncertainty of our text books, is equally applicable to the Scriptures. In these, also, the critic will never find an end; but he who, on the whole, is able to find nourishment and joy in them, will certainly not be troubled upon that account.

A wholly opposite and much more general opinion

* Ibid. p. 20, 21.

is, that the Roman law can and ought to be much
more easily learnt, and that only a short time need
be spent upon it. This opinion is partly theo-
retical; partly (as will presently appear) reduced
into practice, particularly where, on the establishment of new codes, the Roman law was to be no
more than an ancillary pursuit : — the same when
the education of future legislators was the question. The painful study of details was believed to
be useless for these purposes ; people might rest
satisfied with what was termed the spirit of this
law. Now this spirit consists of that which is
otherwise termed Institutes, and which may be
highly useful to begin with ; — the most general
notions and rules without critical examination,
without application, and, most particularly, without resort to original authorities, by which alone
the life and vigour of all is to be preserved. But
this is of no avail, and, unless people are willing
to do more, the little time they devote is entirely
thrown away. The only use such a course of
study can be of, is the preservation of the name
and the outward forms of our science, whereby perhaps their revival at some future better
time may be facilitated. But most particularly

to be deprecated is the notion that a future legislator, for whom, at any rate, this knowledge will be allowed to be important and valuable, could make shift with such a slight gentleman-like acquaintance with it, as is felicitously termed *teinture* by the French. It is precisely for this application to original production, that a far deeper knowledge is necessary than for the ordinary business of the jurist; a man must have made himself thoroughly master of the very letter of the historical materials, to be able to use them freely as an instrument for the exposition of new forms,—or the *sermocinari tanquam e vinculis* is inevitable. Apply this perverted mode of thinking to language, and it would be tantamount to saying that, for everyday intercourse and ordinary life, a man should be well acquainted with its richness, vigour, and variety, but might content himself with a superficial knowledge of it for poetry.

What has here been wished for from the study of the law, is not to be preserved in books, not even to be entrusted to individual lawyers, but to be common to all jurists who will labour in their calling with energy and spirit. A living school ought therefore to be formed, as the aggregate body of Roman jurists, not merely the followers of Sabinius or Proculeius by themselves, actually formed one large school. Moreover, by such hearty co-operation of the whole body of jurists alone, can the few be produced whose genius qualifies them for original invention; and it is a baneful prejudice to suppose that these would constantly spring up, be the condition of the school what it might. The example of Montesquieu is very instructive in this particular : no one can be ignorant of the independent energy with which he strove to free himself from the narrowness of his nation and age. Lawyer as he was by profession, and in a *pays de droit écrit*, and although the Romans have no more zealous worshipper than he, so that neither inclination nor opportunity to become acquainted with the Roman law could be wanting to him ; nevertheless, his knowledge of it was extremely moderate, and whole sections of his work are for that reason wholly unfounded ; of which his history of the Roman Law of Inheritance * may serve as an example. This was the consequence of the total nullity of the juridical school of his time, which he was not able to overcome. Generally speaking, any one may convince himself by the thorough study of literary history, how

* Esprit des Lois, Liv. 27.

little of the phenomena presented by it can be with
truth exclusively ascribed to individuals, independently of the spirit and exertions of the age
and the nation. But this diffusion of legal science
ought to take place, not only amongst the jurists of
the learned class, the teachers and writers, but even
amongst the practical lawyers. And this very approximation of theory and practice it is, from which
the real improvement of the administration of law
must proceed, and in which, particularly, we have
to learn from the Romans ; our theory, too, must become more practical, and our practice more scientific than it has hitherto been. Leibnitz was of
opinion, that the writers of *Concilia* were almost
the only juridical writers who really extended jurisprudence, and enriched it by the observation of new
cases ;* at the same time he expresses a wish, that a
society of about thirty jurists would frame new Pandects, in the shape of an abstract of every thing
truly practical and peculiar in recent authors.† Independently of Leibnitz, but in the same spirit,

* Nova methodus, P. 2. s. 82. [I subjoin the passage: "In
his autoribus laudabile est, quod novos emergentes casus per-
petuæ memoriæ consignant, orbemque juridicum continuâ
auctione locupletant, quod non faciunt autores exercitationum
et commentariorum semper vetera ruminantes."—TRANSL.]

† l. c. s. 85—90.

Möser proposes to form new Pandects, by a systematic collection of the actual law cases of a country.* Both are very plausible; but one indispensable requisite has not been taken into the account,— the capacity for making genuine experiences. For a man must have the clear, lively conception of the whole constantly present to his mind, to enable him to take a practical lesson from the individual case; and once again, therefore, it is the speculative, scientific spirit alone, by which even the practice becomes profitable and instructive. There is, indeed, a unity in this multiformity; but we do not discover it, unless we bring a properly prepared spirit to the examination: nay, without this spirit, we shall not be able to fix with certainty even the individual form of the particulars composing the multiformity. For this reason, every case in the Pandects has a fixed individuality: in reading the judgments of the eighth and ninth centuries, on the contrary, the one sounds exactly like the other, and it is as if the same case had been constantly recurring. Not that the legal relations themselves had really fallen into this degree of uniformity, but the capacity for decision

* Möser's Proposal for a Collection of Indigenous Law Cases. Patriotic Fancies, Th. 2. N. 53. (Third Edit. n. 44.)

was lost, and the more this is wanting, the more unattainable is certain and uniform law. A free communication between the Law-Faculties and the Courts, which has been recently proposed, would be an excellent mode of bringing about this approximation of Theory and Practice. The Law-Faculties, as Courts of Appeal,* were capable of this, and did it well enough originally, after their fashion; but after they became mere manufacturers of judgments, their duty could not fail to be more mechanical than that of the regular courts; nay, it was no longer in the power of enlightened members of the old faculties, to purify this state of things; not to say, that, through the necessary practice of this unprofitable handicraft, the best energies of scientific jurisprudence were withdrawn, and, in part, are still withdrawn from it.* At the same time, this connection of practice with a vigorous constantly-progressing theory, is the only means of gaining a constant supply of men of

---

* [From the time of Maximilian, the immediate predecessor of Charles 5th, the Law-Faculties, consisting of the Professors of the German Universities, have constituted Courts of Appeal in the last resort. The appellants, I believe, may select any University they please; for instance, a case decided in Hanover may be sent to a Prussian University.—TRANSL.]

talent for the Bench. The situation of judge, it is true, may be honourable and respectable without this; he may, moreover, be constantly improving himself by occupations, unconnected with his vocation, such as the disposition of the individual may incline him to ; but it will be a very different matter, should the vocation itself, from its connexion with the whole, assume a scientific character and become itself a means of improvement. Such a state of things alone will satisfy all demands. The individual judge will no longer serve as a mere instrument, but be of a liberal and honourable calling, and the administration of justice will be really and scientifically complete. Even the French have recognized this particular necessity, though in their peculiar and somewhat degrading way.* The most unfavourable state of things, in this respect, is undeniably that, in which the judge is to be tied down to the mechanical application of a given text, which he is not allowed to interpret; if this be considered as the extreme point upon the one

---

* Projet de Code Civil, p. xiii. Dans l'etat de nos sociétés, il est trop heureux que la jurisprudence forme une science qui puisse fixer le talent, flatter l'amour propre, et réveiller l'emulation." P. xiv. " On ne saurait comprendre combien cette habitude de science et de raison adoucit et règle le pouvoir."

side, the extreme point on the other would be, that the judge should have to find the law for every case; all arbitrary discretion, however, being excluded by the certainty resulting from a strict scientific method. But to this second point, it is not impossible to approximate, at least; and, on attaining it, the most ancient judicial organization of Germany would be revived in a renovated form.

I have above assumed three things to be necessary: — law-authorities, ministry of justice, and forms of procedure, all in good condition. How the authorities are to be based on a profound and comprehensive science, has been shown; as also how, by the same means, the ministry of justice may be rendered truly fit for this vocation. But both will be insufficient, if the form of procedure be bad. In this respect many countries of Germany require a speedy and effectual reform. The most common defects are, anarchy of the advocates, abuse of imparlances* and their prolongation, multiplication of appeals, and particularly of appeals to the faculties, which, judi-

* [*Frist* is the period of delay allowed a suitor to appear or plead in. I have not been able to learn what is meant by *Anarchie der Advokaten*, the rank of the German advocate being accurately defined.—TRANSL.]

ciously applied, might prove exceedingly valuable. To remedy these, the aid of legislation will be required; general consultation and communication between the states of Germany on the subject is also highly desirable. Only it is not necessary that one universal form should be generally adopted at once. Let a variety of experiments be made; that which proves to be best, will soon be universally introduced. Between the Prussian procedure and the common procedure hitherto in use, (the ideas of which may be viewed in contrast with each other), there are many intervening gradations, the merits of which experience only can decide.

According to this view, therefore, no code, it is true, would be formed in countries where the common law prevails; but it by no means follows that civil legislation would be altogether dispensed with. Independently of legislative provisions on political grounds (which do not belong to this place), it might be employed for two purposes: the decision of controversies (disputed points), and the recording of old customs. By the legislative decision of controversies, one principal objection would be removed, which, without looking further, people have hitherto supposed to lie against the practical applicability of the Roman law. Besides, these controversies are not so very bad in reality. In the first place, we must not set down as a controversy every instance in which ignorance or stupidity has ever prosecuted an unsuccessful inquiry. In the second place, legislation need not trouble itself with such controversies as do indeed exist in the books, but are seldom forthcoming in practice. Deduct these two descriptions of cases, and much still remains to be done; but the Code Napoleon, young as it is, may already, in this respect, be placed alongside of the Roman law. These controversies, however, had perhaps better be decided in the form of provisional ordinances or directions to the courts, than by regular enactments, since the former would be less likely to prejudice the chance of a better foundation in theory.

The second object of legislation would be the recording of customary law, which might in this manner be subjected to a superintendance, such as that effected by means of the edict in Rome. It is not to be imagined that the code, hitherto opposed, would, after all, be let in in this manner, only under a different name; on the contrary, the difference concerns the very essence of the thing. For in this customary law, that only will be comprised which has been decided in actual practice, and this, now that the legislator has the decisions before him, will, beyond a doubt, be thoroughly comprehended ; the code, on the contrary, is obliged to speak on every subject,—even when there is no immediate motive thereto, and no special observation supplies the requisite capacity,—merely in anticipation of future possible cases. Every one must see that this is not the place for speaking of the mode of carrying into execution the remaining branches of civil legislation.

I have been hitherto considering what course is to be pursued by countries in which the common law prevails, in order to bring the law into a satisfactory state. I now proceed to state the higher object, which is attainable by the same course. Let jurisprudence be once generally diffused amongst the jurists in the manner above-mentioned, and we again possess, in the legal profession, a subject for living customary law,—consequently, for real improvement ; the practice of our courts of justice was but a clumsy substitute for this customary law ; the practice of the law-faculties the clumsiest of all. The historical matter of law, which now hems us in on all sides, will then be brought under subjection, and constitute our wealth. We shall then possess a truly national law, and a powerful expressive language will not be wanting to it. We may then give up the Roman law to history, and we shall have, not merely a feeble imitation of the Roman system, but a truly national and new system of our own. We shall have reached somewhat higher than to a merely sure and speedy administration of justice; that state of clear perceptiveness which is ordinarily peculiar to the law of young nations, will be combined with the height of scientific developement. Then too, may future degenerate times be provided for, and then will be the time for considering whether this be done best by codes or in another form. I do not say that this state of things will ever arrive; this depends upon the combination of the rarest and most fortunate circumstances. What we jurists can contribute towards it, is, an openness to conviction, and honest hearty co-operation; after doing so, we may quietly attend the result; but, above all, we must avoid destroying that which may advance us towards the object in view.

When the Jews at Mount Sinai were tired of waiting for the laws of God, they framed, in their impatience, a golden calf, and the genuine tables of the law were broken to pieces thereupon.

IX.—WHAT IS TO BE DONE WHERE CODES EXIST ALREADY.

I now come to those countries of Germany, in which codes exist already; it is clear that only the Prussian Landrecht and the Austrian Gesetzbuch can be comprised under this head; not the French code, which must be regarded as a subdued political malady, from which indeed we shall still feel many evil consequences.

I have already given my opinion on these German codes, but I should be misunderstood were I supposed to think their abrogation desirable. On the contrary, they are rather to be treated as occurrences new and unprecedented in the history of law, and their abrogation would not merely be followed by great confusion, but, what is more, the sudden abrogation of that which had been only just completed with the best intentions and great exertions, could not fail of having a baneful effect on the public mind. Besides, a large proportion of the evil which a general code would produce, is not to be apprehended from these, so long as the common law is left in other countries of Germany. There is, therefore, no question about their repeal—but the first consideration is, how to avoid the evils which were let in by the injudicious treatment of the codes.

He who is convinced by what has been said above of the nature and origin of our codes, will not doubt, that the same historically-grounded course of legal study, which was necessary before their introduction, has not become in the slightest de_ gree less necessary through them; and that it is idle to think that, on their account, a man may now put up with a superficial exposition of the pre-existing law. This continuing necessity is, with regard to the immediate application, more pressing in respect of the Austrian Gesetz-buch; but, for other reasons, it exists no less in respect of the Prussian Landrecht. The often-cherished hope, therefore, that the study of law may be rendered easier and simpler by codes, is vain. Unless this is to be faulty and insufficient with reference to the established state of the law (for then any degree of simplification is possible), the whole of the former labour remains, and to this is added a new one, which, by reason of the destruction of the original form, is even more embarrassing than the old. But not only is the former course of study indispensable for the thorough knowledge and application of the codes, but also for the improving and maturing of them, which every one must admit to be necessary, how highly soever he may estimate their merits. For the codes themselves are framed upon scientific principles, and can only be safely examined, purified, and perfected upon such. A mere board of professional men, who, from the nature of their calling and the multiplicity of their duties, are compelled to limit their active intercourse with the science or theory of law, is not sufficient for this purpose. Even the constant examination of the Gesetzbuch consequent on the attention paid by the courts to its application, is valuable certainly, but not enough; many defects will probably be discovered in this mode of proceeding, but the mode itself is casual, and just as many defects might not be touched by it. Theory does not stand altogether in the same relation to practice, as a sum in arithmetic to its proof.

It is interesting to consider how the study has been viewed and ordered in the states where codes have been established. On this subject, the state of things in France and the present system of the Parisian Law Schools, may be again referred to.* To this school are attached three professors for the Code, one for Procedure, one for the Roman Law,—and every school is to have the same. But Paris has, besides, two particular chairs, for the *code civil approfondi* and for the *code de commerce.* Criminal Law and Criminal Procedure, Legal History, and old French Law, are not read. Each Professor regularly gives a course of a year's duration (deducting three months' vacation in Paris, and two months' vacation in all other places) consisting of three lectures of an hour and a half each a week; the lectures are every where of the same length. The code, therefore, is taught in three of these courses, each professor taking only a third part of the whole. Each Professor has a *suppléant,* who supplies his place when he is prevented from lecturing. Berthelot lectured on the Roman Law,—on the Institutes of Heineccius, to which he had added a French translation, to assist the comprehension of his auditors; since the death of Berthelot, his former *suppléant,* Blondeau,† lectures on it, but, what

* I use the MS. and oral communications of a Doctor of this School.

† [The present distinguished Dean of the Faculty of Paris, author of many valuable works on jurisprudence.—TRANS.]

is hardly credible, on the code, pointing out the variations, article by article. The bachelor must have studied two years, the Licentiate three, the Doctor four; the Roman Law course is prescribed to the first, the repetition of that course is discretionary in the second, but positively enjoined to the third; though, strange to say, it is only the repetition of the same institutes with the same professor. After the details that have been given, it will not be necessary to adduce more reasons against this plan of study; but the dilemma in which we are placed, is particularly worthy of remark.

The redactors, themselves, have often declared, that the Code is not sufficient for practical purposes, but that the supplemental aid of science is necessary for these. And yet all the scientific education exclusively refers to the Code, for the little Roman Law that is taught, is really not worth reckoning. What, then, is this science based upon? Undoubtedly, on the practice of the courts, that very practice, the diversities of which it was the great object to remove, and which has lost all consideration by the dissolution of the old courts, and the confounding

of their jurisdictions. That such a state of things
is never stationary, but constantly retrograding,
is palpable. It is natural that, in every age, the
state of jurisprudence should be determined by
the quality of that which the age in question actually (though not always avowedly) considers and
treats as the immediate object of study ; jurisprudence will always be some what (and perhaps much)
more deeply rooted than this object. Thus, for example, the first glossarists had the advantage of being
compelled to draw from the authorities themselves ;
— these, therefore, were their object. Bartholus,
on the contrary, had the writings of the glossarists,
which by his time had established themselves between the cotemporary jurists and the authorities ;
and this is one great reason for his school's being
so much inferior to that of the glossarists. The
same retrogradation will invariably occur, where
the principle of following up everything to its root
is not observed, which principle has been already
described as the characteristic of the historical
method. Thus then, also, with regard to the code ;
any one of the redactors, granting him to entertain
the highest possible opinion of the code, would notwithstanding believe in his heart, that he himself
stands higher than his work ; he would allow that he

is in no respect indebted to the code for his own acquirements and capacity, and that the present generation, which is to be educated by means of the code, would never reach the height on which he himself stands, and standing on which he was capable of producing such a work. This simple reflection will lead to the same result in all cases, where, on the introduction of a new code, the preceding studies are destroyed; which is like breaking down the bridge upon which one has crossed the stream.

The new Austrian study-ordinance (of 1810) unites the juridical and political studies into one whole; which is completed in four years, three hours a-day being set apart for the lectures during the whole period.* Each subject of study is only lectured upon once. German law is not included; undoubtedly because it was little known in Austria,

* In these the following are employed as authorities: Instruction zur Ausführung des Lehrplanes, &c. im. 35-ten. Bande von K. Franz 1. Gesetzsammlung.—A. von Hess encycl. methodol. Einleitung in das juridisch-politische Studium. Wien und Triest, 1813. 8. It appears (p. 9.) that the documents relating to the plan of study have been communicated to the writer, so that his *exposé des motifs* may be regarded in some measure as official.

even before the establishment of the Gesetzbuch. On the other hand, the Roman law is certainly taught, and the reasons which led to its being included in the plan, are of the most excellent and liberal description. The first is, the derivation of the new Gesetzbuch from the Roman law: the second, that the pre-existing common law (and particularly the Roman part of it) stands in the same relation to every positive system of jurisprudence, as the ancient languages to general education, i. e. as the scientific element, properly so termed, whereby our calling acquires a scientific character, and, at the same time, as the common tie between jurists of different countries.* This view, which is beyond a doubt that of the study-committee itself,† certainly merits the highest approbation ; however, I cannot but doubt whether the means enumerated are sufficient for this avowed object. The professor of the Roman law, it is true, is to begin by laying down a history of it, and endeavour to teach the pupil "the system in its fundamental principles and from the autho-

* Hess. s. 16.

† S. V. s. 141. [The *Studien-commission* is a board of public instruction, exercising, I understand, a most despotic and baneful control over every branch of education.—TRANS.]

rities,"* but with the limited time prescribed, it is absolutely impossible to go through more than the ordinary institutes; as, for the whole branch, only a course of half a year at two hours a day (according to private accounts, in fact nine hours a week) is allowed,—the very same time as in Paris. Any man may easily compute how much can be done in so short a period : besides, a manual for the lectures upon this plan has already appeared,† from which it is easy to see how unsatisfactory this system of instruction cannot fail to be, — and really without any fault on the part of the author, whose diligence and knowledge of the recent progress of jurisprudence merit really the highest commendation. It would only be necessary to become convinced of the insufficiency of this plan, and to consult, without prejudice, the experience of other countries of Germany ; there would be no want of means for a different arrangement, and, least of all, of time. According to the computation of the plan, each student is to attend three hours a day : if five hours be substi-

* Hess, s. 40, 41.

† Kaufmann's Introduction to the Roman Civil Law. First Part. Vienna and Triest, 1814. 8vo.

tuted, sixteen courses would be gained in four years, and, in that case, not only might all branches of knowledge, indispensable to scientific instruction, be taught, but the principal subjects might be lectured on by a greater number of professors, by which alone true life is infused into the studies of the universities. It certainly was thought that five hours a-day according to the locality, is too much ; it being, for example, too great an exertion to attend three hours consecutively ;* but on this point I rely upon the experience of other German universities, where this never causes the slightest difficulty. I will say nothing of there being universities where many students attend from ten to eleven hours a-day, for this, even where it is followed, is admitted to be an injurious practice, which efforts are making to oppose.

In the Prussian states, ever since the establishment of the Landrecht, no order of study has ever been prescribed, and this freedom from restraint, sanctioned by the former experience of the German universities, has never been infringed upon. Even the number of professors, formerly required on account of the common law, has not been reduced, and the curators of the universities have never led either

* Egger's Anhang zu Hess, p. 93.

the professors or the students to believe, that a part of the lectures, formerly necessary, were likely to be dispensed with. Originally it was thought advisable, that, in each university, one chair at least should be set apart for the Prussian law, and a considerable prize was offered for the best manual.* But even this was subsequently no longer required, and up to the present time the Prussian law has not been taught at the university of Berlin. The established examinations are formed upon the same principle; the first, on the entrance into real matters of business, turning exclusively on the common law: the next period is set apart for the directly-practical education of the jurisconsult, and the two following examinations are the first that have the Landrecht for their subject-matter, at the same time, however, without excluding the common law. At present, therefore, juridical education is considered to consist of two halves; the first half (the university) including only the learned groundwork, the second, on

* Introduction to the plan of the Code, Th. 2. Abthl. 3.

† There is a very instructive essay on this subject by the minister of justice, Von Kircheisen, in *Mathis jurist. Monatschrift*, B. 4. 65.

the other hand, having for its object the knowledge
of the Landrecht, the knowledge of the Prussian
procedure, and practical skill. The shortening
of the first half according to convenience, has not
been provided against by a special ordinance, but
it has been done in effect by, in the first place,
the prescribed Triennium,* the application of this
time, as is but right, being left to the option of the
professor; secondly, by the ordinance command-
ing that, in all cases of admission to the service of
the state, even the testimonial of the university
professor, and the early school-testimonial, be referred to. We must consider with what earnestness and exertion the Landrecht has been framed,
to feel how much honour is due to this experiment of the Prussian government. For even
with the firm conviction that the new system is an
unqualified improvement, they have refrained, with
honourable timidity, from interfering with the
firmly-rooted scientific custom, which was gradually formed and developed by the wants and intelligence of the times. The sound views of

* The rescripts on this subject, of 1804, 1809 and 1812,
are to be found in the following places : Mathis Monatschrift,
B. 1. S. 56. 61 : B. 8. S. 352. 462. Kampz Monatschrift,
Ileft 1. S. 18.

the Kammergericht* likewise deserve honourable mention; at whose suggestion, in 1801, the use of Latin manuals was prescribed to the law-faculties, because, since the introduction of German manuals, the technical language of the law had become less familiar to jurisconsults;† still this object might have been more safely and completely attained by means of the authorities, than by manuals. As to what particularly concerns the lectures on the Landrecht, I believe that they could not, as things stand, be improved; the later lectures being sufficient to meet the demands of practice, though it might have been very difficult to give the subject a scientific character, for want of special historical authorities. It might possibly be otherwise, were the wish above-expressed, for a free access to the materials of the Landrecht, to be fulfilled.

If, once again, we consider the three Codes above-named together, and with particular reference to the study of the law, it is clear that a peculiar scientific spirit cannot spring from them, and that, even co-existently with them, a scientific spirit will only be kept alive in proportion as the

* [Supreme Court of Judicature. TRANSL.]

† Stengel's Beyträge, B. 13. p. 214. 218.

historical authorities of these Codes remain the constant object of all juridical studies. The same, however, could not fail to be the case, should we resolve on framing a Code for Germany. Thibaut, who advises this, does not wish (as may easily be collected from himself) to do away with scientific jurisprudence; indeed, he expects it to be greatly improved. He does not clearly explain what is to form the basis of the future law-studies, whether (as in Prussia) the old authorities, or (as in France and Austria) the new Code itself; but the last appears to be his opinion.* If this be so, however, I intreat any one to reflect whether a real, living, jurisprudence can possibly be founded upon one of the three new Codes, independently of the sources of the pre-existing law, and of these Codes themselves. But whoever does not believe this to be possible with them, cannot maintain the possibility of it with respect to the proposed Code. For, upon grounds already mentioned, I hold it to be quite impossible for this code to turn out differently from the existing Codes; not merely in the avoiding of particular defects (which is certainly conceivable), but generi-

* Thibaut, Vid. p. 29—32.

cally. Without such a generic difference, however, there will always be the same incompetency for the establishment of an independent jurisprudence. What will then come to pass, it is not difficult to foresee. Either we shall have no juridical literature at all, or (which is more likely) so spiritless, mechanical and intolerable a one as had begun to overwhelm us during the reign of the Code, and we shall then experience all the disadvantages of a refined and complicated system, based upon a demand for science, without being indemnified by any of its characteristic advantages. Nay, to sum up all in a word, it is not improbable that the state of the law amongst us would be even worse than in France; for the striving after a scientific foundation is not one of the national tendencies of the French; but it is clearly one of ours, and so deeply rooted a want is not to be slighted with impunity.

If, on the other hand, it were resolved, even co-existently with the new Code, to found the jurisprudence on the old authorities, the difficulties before-mentioned would occur, and the study, instead of being simplified, would be rendered more complex and less profitable; thus contravening the real object in view. It might possibly be thought that the result would be precisely the same as that which we all know to have been the result of an experiment of the same sort in Prussia, where undoubtedly the *personal* of the administration of justice is excellent, and possesses and merits universal esteem ; but I regard this expectation, also, as an empty delusion. For, in considering it, two circumstances are not to be overlooked, which might well render the result less favourable in other countries : first, that the general character of the Prussian institutions is in accordance with this particular one, and rectifies its practical operation, which would hardly be the case in other countries of Germany : secondly, however, and in a far greater degree—that, in the Prussian states themselves, the condition of the law would be completely changed by the code proposed for the rest of Germany. For the ground-work of the legal knowledge of the Prussian jurists is laid at the Universities, consequently, through the sources of the common law : the studies of the Universities, therefore, constitute, together with those of the other German universities, one entire system. But it is impossible to say how much vigour these studies derive from the circumstance of their sources being in force as law in the rest of Germany, and how its strength and spirit would gradually disappear, should these sources cease to be any where of direct authority. Then, therefore, even as regards the Prussian states, the study of jurisprudence would be weakened by the Code, nor do I understand how the experience of Prussia up to the present time can ensure us against the apprehended evil.

———————

X.—GENERAL OBSERVATIONS.

The result of these considerations is, that the scientific study of the law, being that on which its preservation and improvement exclusively depend, must be the same in both sorts of countries, as well those that have codes, as those that have not. What is more, I do not limit this general effect to the common law; on the contrary, it cannot fail to be extended to the provincial laws, — for two reasons. First, because the provincial laws are, for the most part, only intelligible by comparison and reference to the old national roots; secondly, because every thing relating to the history of the

individual countries of Germany has a natural interest for the whole nation. It is undeniable that
the provincial laws have, up to the present time,
been least of any cultivated in this manner;* but
there are many reasons for expecting a more general interest in German history for the future, and
even the study of the provincial laws will have
new life infused into it thereby ; which, indeed, no
less than the common law, ought not to be permitted to become merely mechanical. And thus
my plan tends, by a different way, to the same object, which the advocates of the general code are
aiming at ; viz. the making the law the concern of
the nation at large, and, at the same time, a
new confirmation of its unity. Only my plan
is more comprehensive, including, as it does,
all the countries of Germany ; whilst, through the
proposed Code, Germany would be broken up into
three great districts, the divisions of which would,
by means of the law, become still more strongly
marked than before; namely, Austria, Prussia,
and the countries of the Code. †

* Thibaut, p. 27, 28.

† The present proposals for the establishment of a new code
are exclusively attributable to the condition of the countries,
in which, up to the present time, the common law or the Code

The recognising and presupposing of this community of the law in all existing institutions, then, I hold, on account of that very union to be founded on it, to be one of the most important concerns of the nation. As there is no Prussian or Bavarian, but a German, language or literature, just so is it with the remote sources of our laws and the historical investigation of them. That it is so, is not owing to the arbitrary fiat of a prince, nor can any prince prevent it,—only it may be mistaken; but every mistake as to that which really belongs to the nation at large, and is falsely treated as peculiar to the individual race, is fraught with ruin.

If, then, we look around us in search of a mean whereby this common study may be established and forwarded, we find one,—not of arbitrary invention, but prepared for ages by the wants of the nation,— in the universities. The deepening of the foundations of our law, and particularly that

was in force, and I have tacitly assumed that the proposal itself is not more extended than the occasion which gave birth to it. Were Austria and Prussia, however, to be also comprised in it, this comprehensiveness would certainly be highly commendable in a political point of view, but, as regards these countries themselves, it would be well to consider what was said above (c. 4.), with reference to other considerations, against the abrogation of their codes.

of Germany at large, for which most remains to be done, is not only to be expected from these, but also to be solemnly required. But in order that they may be found equal to the call, a wish must be fulfilled, which will doubtless meet with the hearty concurrence of those to whom my views have been hitherto opposed. Austria, Bavaria, and Wirtemberg, those excellent, purely German races,* have not (partly from of old, partly at present) that freedom of intercourse, as regards their universities, with the rest of Germany, which is so highly advantageous to the other countries; this intercourse is impeded, partly by custom, partly by restrictive enactments. The experience of the period that has just elapsed, has shown what confidence the nations of Germany may place in each other, and that their only safety is in the closest union. The time therefore appears to be arrived, for this intercouse to be not merely established, but favoured and encouraged in every way; no one can think it dangerous now, and every one must see how admirably it may operate towards the fraternization of nations. But not only in a political point of view, would this unrestricted and frequent intercourse be of

* [Austria is not generally regarded in this light.—Transl.]

the highest importance, but still more so for the intrinsic scientific excellence of the universities themselves. As in the general commerce of the world, a bad monetary system of a particular state cannot be long maintained without being felt and detected by the bad consequences resulting from it,—in the same manner would any faulty regulation of a single university be soon observed and remedied through this desired intercourse; all the universities would mutually support and exalt each other, and the experience of one would be the common property of all.

XI.—THIBAUT'S PROPOSAL.

THIBAUT assures us, in the beginning of his work, that he speaks as a warm friend of his country, and he has certainly a right to say so. For, at the time of the Code, he maintained the honour of German jurisprudence in a series of articles, whilst many were hailing the new wisdom — many, the very despotism to which it led—with senseless jubilees. The object of his proposal, also, the firmer and closer union of the nation, is an additional proof of the goodness of his intentions, which I acknowledge with pleasure. Up to this point, therefore, we are agreed, and our contest therefore is not a hostile one; we have the same object earnestly at heart, and are deliberating about the means. As to these means, however, our views differ very widely indeed. Much relating to them had been said in the course of this work; the precise proposal itself is now to be investigated.

Thibaut assumes that the proposed code may be formed in two, three, four years, not as a mere make-shift, but as a finished work, which may descend to our children and our children's children as a sacred bequest, and which, even in future times, would only require altering in particular parts. He by no means thinks the task an easy one; on the contrary, he thinks it the most difficult of all things. The principal question naturally is, who is to execute the work? and on this point it is highly important not to permit ourselves to be led astray by exaggerated expectations of the present, but to estimate, quietly and impartially, what faculties we have at command. Thibaut also has done this: we must reckon on two classes of

M

labourers, practical men, and jurists of the learned
order; and both, of course, are required by him.
But his expectations from the practical men are
very moderate; and, from certain indications, it
would seem that he founds no extraordinary hope
upon the learned. For this very reason he demands a committee for the work—not one person,
nor a few, but many and of all countries are to
frame the code.

There are certainly affairs of life in which six
men do just six times as much as one, others in
which they do more, but others again in which
they do much less. Now the code is a description of work, in which the united force of many
will be by no means a proportionally augmented
force. What is more, it can never be really well
executed in this manner, and for the simple reason, that, from its nature, it is neither a single decision, nor an aggregate of single decisions, but
an organic whole. A bench of judges is practicable, because the opinions for condemnation
or acquittal can be given and counted in each individual case. That the preparation of the code
has nothing in common with this, is self-evident.
To refer to a preceding remark—amongst the Romans in Papinian's time, a code was possible, be-

cause their aggregate juridical literature constituted an organic whole : it might be said (to use an expression of the later jurists) that at that time the individual jurists were *fungible* persons. In such a state of things indeed, there were many ways leading to a good code: one jurist might frame it, and the others afterwards supply particular defects; which was practicable, because each individual jurist was then entitled to rank as the representative of the juridical cultivation of the time ; or several, independently of each other, might each work out the whole, and by collating and combining their productions a new one might be formed, more complete than each taken singly, but homogeneous with all.

Now I ask every one to compare our condition with this, which is, in this respect, its exact opposite. To begin with the least important particular — let any man run over in his mind a number of the jurists now living, and ask himself, whether the existing law could be so much as systematized by their combined labours ;—he would soon be convinced of the utter impossibility. But that a code is a much greater work, and that a higher degree of organic unity must be required of it, is what no one will deny. In reality, therefore, the code,—if it is not to be a mere lifeless, mechanical, and, consequently, worthless composition,— could not be framed by such a committee, but only by an individual; the others would only be able to afford a subordinate description of aid, by communicating their advice and opinions on the occurrence of particular doubts, or by exerting themselves to purify the work when completed, by the detection of individual defects. But whoever admits this, must, as regards the present age, despair of the practicability of the proposal; for to find that same individual, the true law-giver, is perfectly impossible, because, by reason of the heterogeneous character of the modes of thought and knowledge of our jurists, no individual can be treated as the representative of the species.

Should any one still believe in the possibility of the code being actually framed by a committee, let him have the goodness to read so much as a single section of the discussions of the French *Conseil d'Etat,* which Thibaut has so truly delineated. I doubt not that our discussions would be better in many parts; but, at the risk of being accused of partiality to the French, I cannot suppress the conviction, that ours would be in other respects inferior to this prototype.

It has frequently been wished, that the code should be popular, and Thibaut also once refers to the demand. Properly understood, this demand may be complied with. For language, the most effective medium by which a communication of mind can take place, also checks and limits this mental intercourse in many ways. The best part of thought is frequently absorbed by this medium, in consequence of the incapacity either of the speaker or the hearer. But by natural ability or art this medium may be brought under such command, that neither sort of incapacity is any longer an obstacle. The thought passes over the varying characters and capacities of the listeners, and hits them in the common intellectual centre point. Then is it that the high are satisfied, while all is clear even to the low; both see the thought above them, in an elevated improving point of view; and it is within the reach of both. Thus, there was somewhere a miraculous image of Christ, which had the property of being a hand's breadth taller than the tallest man who might place himself beside it; were it a man of moderate size, or a little man, that came, the difference was still the same, never greater. This simple, truly popular style is to be seen (to speak only of our native literature) in our better sort of chronicles, but it may also appear in many other forms. Should we once regain it, many an excellent thing will be possible; amongst others, a good historical style, and, amongst others, a popular code.

XII.—CONCLUSION.

I SHALL sum up in a few words in what my view agrees with that of the advocates of a code, and in what they differ.

We are agreed as to the end in view: we desire a sound system of law, secure against the encroachments of caprice and dishonesty; as also, the unity of the nation, and the concentration of its scientific efforts upon the same object. For this end, *they* are anxious for a code, which, however, would only produce the desired unity for one half of Germany, and separate the rest by a line of demarcation, more strongly marked than before—*I* see the proper means in an organically progressive jurisprudence, which may be common to the whole nation.

In the opinions we form of our present condition,

also, we coincide, for we both regard it as defective.
They, however, see the cause of the evil in the
sources of law, and believe that they could remedy
it by a code—*I*, on the other hand, find it in
ourselves, and believe, for this very reason, that
we are not qualified to frame a code. The words of
one of the most distinguished Germans of the sixteenth century, would almost seem to have been
spoken in our time : *

" Nam mihi aspicienti legum libros, et cognita
pericula Germaniæ, sæpe totum corpus cohor-
rescit, cum reputo quanta incommoda secutura
sint, si Germania propter bella amitteret hanc
eruditam doctrinam juris et hoc curjæ orna-
mentum . . . Non igitur deterreamur periculis,
non frangamur animis, ... nec possessionem
studii nostri deseramus. —— Itaque Deus flectat
animos principum ac potentum ad hujus doctrinæ
conservationem, magnopere decet optare bonos et
prudentes. Nam hac remota, ne dici potest
quanta in aulis tyrannis, in judiciis barbaries, de-
nique confusio in tota civili vita secutura esset,
quam ut Deus prohibeat, ex animo petamus.

* Melanchthon, Oratio de dignitate legum ; in select. decla-
mat. T. 1. Servestæ 1587. p. 247. und Or. de vita Irnerii et
Bartoli. T. 2. p. 411.

APPENDIX I.

[The first Appendix, as stated in the Author's Preface, consists of an article originally published in the *Zeitschrift für geschichtliche Rechtwissenschaft*, in 1816. It contains a summary of all the opinions pronounced up to that time for or against Codification ;—those of Thibaut, Feuerbach, Pfeiffer, Almendigen, and some anonymous writers, *for*—Hugo, Schrader, and some anonymous writers, *against* — with a running commentary, and a few concluding observations, by the author. It is beside my purpose to translate this article, which is thirty closely printed pages in length; nor does it comprise anything very striking or new, if we except the proposition with which Savigny winds up. He states that a comprehensive manual *(handbuch)* is what the German jurists are most in want of, and, admitting that no one jurist would be equal to the composition of it, he thinks that by the co-operation of all " who have an inward call for the undertaking," such a manual might within a few years be produced. Lest the term *manual* should deceive the reader, I think it right to add that the contribution of each particular collaborator is to comprise, not merely the positive rules, but the history, science, and literature, nay, even all the theories and speculations, connected with the subject entrusted to him. To insure the uniformity of the work, the author recommends a constant communication to be kept up between all who may engage in it. " Such an undertaking must infallibly succeed, were it only set about without egotism, or personal assumption, in pure love for the thing. It would be a fine example of public spirit, were qualified jurists of the most opposite opinions, friends and enemies of new codes, willing to combine for this end, and the effective co-operation of Thibaut, for every reason but more particularly for this, would be of the highest importance. Complaints have frequently, and with justice, been made, that the Germans, kept asunder by idle irreconcileable conceits, would have no object in common: here then is a common object, exactly adapted to our capacity, and for which the co-operation of governments is not at all, or very incidentally, required. Legislation will be as much facilitated as science thereby, and even those, who hope for salvation from codes, cannot fail to see their object advanced by it."

I own myself totally unable to reconcile the confidence with which the author looks forward to the consummation of this plan, with what he says in the work (ante p. 179.) as to the low state of juridical learning in Germany, and the unfitness of cotemporary jurists to systematize the existing law.

Savigny lays so much stress on the second Appendix, that I am induced to print it entire.—TRANSL.]

APPENDIX II.

Analyse des observations des tribunaux d'appel et du tribunal de cassation sur le projet de code civil (von Crussaire). Paris 1802. p. 5—9.

MONTPELLIER. Il faut au Code un caractère de simplicité que n'offre pas le projet : jamais la France ne fut dans une situation plus heureuse pour recevoir une législation simple.

Dans l'état où la législation projettée se présente, les formes y semblent quelquefois un peu trop compliquées. Il est à craindre qu'en trompant le voeu exprimé dans le Discours préliminaire, le fisc n'ait autant à gagner que le justiciable à perdre.

Quant aux choses, les circonstances et les localités sont et doivent être la règle nécessaire et le motif déterminant de la loi ; telles sont, par exemple, les lois agraires, toutes celles qui ont trait à l'agriculture,. aux servitudes réelles, services fonciers, etc. Ces lois sont tellement modifiées par les localités, que celles qui sont appropriées à une contrée, pays plat, ne conviennent pas souvent à la contrée voisine, pays montagneux.

D'après ces principes, comment concevoir un systême de législation uniforme sur l'usage des eaux pour l'irrigation des terres, et l'exploitation des usines, sans nulle distinction, entre les propriétés et contre l'usage des lieux, qui ne se régle pas toujours d'apres l'utilité (ainsi que l'établit le projet) mais bien d'aprés la propriété qui en est acquise exclusivement, à ceux qui sont en droit de s'en servir.

Le même inconvenient se présente à l'égard de l'exploitation, et la durée des baux à ferme et à cheptel qui, dans certains pays, comportent *equitablement* des stipulations que le projet de code proscrit.

Il en est de même des servitudes rurales dont l'usage, non moins fréquent que varié, ne peut pas sans doute s'arranger, comme dans le projet de code, dans le cadre d'un *systême uniforme*. Les exceptions doivent être à côté de la régle, et dictées par la connaissance exacte des localités.

Dire que la disposition générale du projet de code pourvoit à ces inconvéniens, en laissant les anciens usages derriére les nouvelles lois, ce n'est pas se pénétrer assez de la difficulté à l'égard de tous les cas. Il y a aussi d'autres usages généraux qui ont divisés la France en deux grandes parties, en pays de droit écrit, et en pays de coutume ; ces usages se confondent, par le projet de code, dans l'unité du même systême ; c'est, dit-on, une *transaction* entre *le droit ecrit* et *les coutumes*.

Pour apprécier cette *transaction* et les avantages qui doivent en resulter pour l'un et l'autre pays, il faut faire quelques remarques :

1. Ce qui s'est trouvé réformé par la force des choses, et par la constitution même, n'a pu faire l'objet de cette transaction.

D'un autre côté, dans les lois romaines, comme dans les coutumes, il faut distinguer celles qui ont pour fondement le droit naturel et l'équité, de celles qui tiennent à la fois à l'ordre naturel et civil, ainsi qu'à l'ordre politique ; aux simples rapports des individus entre eux, et à ces mêmes rapports compliqués, avec ceux de la société ; les premières, d'une équité évidente, ne peuvent pas être maniée au gré du législateur ; les autres se prêtent à l'esprit de système qui crée les différentes combinaisons parmi lesquelles le législateur peut choisir celui qui lui paraît le plus convenable.

C'est ainsi que les rédacteurs du projet de code ont eu à choisir entre les dispositions du *droit écrit* et les dispositions du *droit coutumier*, principalement sur les points systématiques *de la puissance paternelle, des tutelles, minorités et interdictions, des successions, des donations entre-vifs ou à cause de mort, dés droits des époux dans le contrat de marriage, des prescriptions, etc.;* c'est là où l'on met le droit romain plus aux prises et en oppositions avec les coutumes, et où l'on a pu le faire *transiger.*

Mais qu'a-t-il été accordé ou soustrait au *droit écrit?* Qu'a-t-il été accordé ou soustrait au *droit coutumier?*

Quant à la *puissance paternelle,* la coutume obtient de l'affaiblir en plaçant à côté d'elle la communauté de biens entre époux; ce qui met en opposition, dans un ménage, le *credit* d'un époux avec l'autorité de l'autre; autorité qui perd presque toute la force qu'elle tient du droit écrit, par l'avantage accordé à la coutume d'ôter aux pères la faculté d'exhéréder leurs enfans, de disposer librement de leurs biens, et d'ôter aux enfans le droit d'exiger des pères un établissement convenable.

Si, dans les *tutelles,* le *droit écrit* l'a emporté dans sa disposition peu convenable à nos usages concernant la division de la tutelle en quatre espèces, la coutume a triomphé dans les points bien plus essentiels où elle ne laisse pas distinguer entre tuteur et curateur, ni entre pupille, et mineur ou adulte, elle a triomphé encore en mettant, à la place de l'interdiction pour cause de prodigalité, la disposition officieuse si peu propre à la remplacer.

Dans les *successions* on ne trouve plus ces grands traits de la législation romaine, qui ne déférait l'hérédité qu'à un seul titre universel par la volonté de l'homme, et à défaut par la disposition de la loi; principe simple dont les avantages étaient sentis dans la pratique.

En écartant ce principe, la coutume fait concourir à la fois la succession légitime avec la succession testamentaire: et il y a tout autant de titres universels qu'il y a de dispositions sur des portions de biens par quelques actes que ce soit. Le

partage en deux lignes pour les ascendans et les collatéraux,
contrarie, dans la plupart des cas, l'équitable disposition du
droit écrit, en faisant passer les biens dans les familles
étrangères ; système qui, par la prolongation des deux lignes
à l'infini, priva les époux de tous les avantages que le droit
écrit leur ménageait sur leur succession réciproque.

Il est vrai que ce droit parait avoir été adopté pour les
prescriptions ; mais ces règles qui ne font que compliquer mal
à propos les dispositions, n'auraient pas dû être maintenues.

Ce serait donc aiusi qu'on aurait fait transiger les deux
droits en laissant à l'empire de la coutume, la presque to-
talité des points sur lesquels elle pourrait être en concurrence
avec le droit romain, et en abandonnant au droit écrit les
autres points qui sont de peu d'importance, droit d'ailleurs
qui était modifié par les coutumes particulières qui y déro-
geaient, ou y ajoutaient selon les convenances ou les localités.

Ainsi, tel pourra être le sort de ce pays que, par le
nouveau système de législation, ils seront frustrés à la fois et
des dispositions du droit écrit, et de celles de leur coutume
particulière, qui leur étaient convenables; et qu'ils recevront,
à la place de ces lois qu'ils avaient choisies, des dispositions
coutumières qui ne leur conviennent pas, et des dispositions
du droit écrit déjà par eux rejettées ou modifiées.

Mais, quelles que soient les nouvelles lois qui seront
données à la France, le législateur ne doit pas moins se tenir
en garde contre les effets de la rétroactivité, et contre les inconvéniens du point de rencontre des nouvelles lois avec les
lois anciennes, pour le prévenir, autant qu'il est possible, ou
les corriger sans blesser la justice et l'équité.

Le projet de Code qui établit en principe *que le loi ne dispose
que pour l'avenir, et qu'elle n'a point d'effet rétroactif* man-
quera le but au moins sur divers cas: par exemple, à l'égard
du cours d'eau, dont l'ancien droit ne permettait pas l'usage
au propriétaire riverain, sur le seul fondement de son utilité
particulière, lorsque l'usage exclusif en était légitimement
acquis à d'autres propriétaires ou possesseurs d'usine ; c'est
ainsi que l'ancien propriétaire se trouverait dépouillé, en
vertu de la loi nouvelle, d'un droit acquis depuis des siècles,

et après avoir fait, sous la foi de l'ancienne loi, des constructions qui lui deviendraient inutiles après la perte de son droit.

Le tribunal de Montpellier desire aussi que le législateur s'explique enfin sur le vrai sens et sur l'effet que doit avoir le décret du...... Septembre 1791, qui déclare non écrites toutes clauses insérées aux actes, et qui seraient contraires aux moeurs, ou aux lois nouvelles, à la liberté religieuse, naturelle et civile, et à celle de se marier ou remarier : et la loi des 24. Octobre et 14. Novembre 1792, qui prohibe les substitutions pour l'avenir, abolit celles qui se trouvaient alors établies, et maintient l'effet de celles seulement qui étaient ouvertes à cette époque.

Les tribunaux ont pensé que le législateur n'avait pas vu d'effets rétroactifs dans ces deux lois; cependant le tribunal de cassation croit y voir ce vice. Le projet de Code ne règle rien à cet égard : or, il serait à desirer que le législateur s'expliquât pour faire cesser ce conflit, et les incertitudes qui en résultent.

Ici, les lacunes qui résulteront de l'abrogation des lois anciennes, générales ou particulières, et locales, présenteront une foule de difficultés à la sagacité du législateur.

Ainsi, régler les rapports, combler les lacunes, régulariser les effets compliqués des anciennes et nouvelles lois ; suppléer à leur silence, pénétrer leur obscurité, telle est la tâche immense qu'impose le perfectionnement du grand ouvrage de la législation nouvelle.

C'est cette tâche que les rédacteurs du projet semblent renvoyer à l'arbitrage des juges pour la remplir, à mesure qu'ils feront l'application des lois aux cas particuliers ; et telle se rait la jurisprudence qu'on entend placer à côté du sanctuaire des lois !

Mais quelle jurisprudence ! n'ayant d'autre règle que l'arbitraire sur l'immensité d'objets à co-ordonner au système de législation nouvelle, à quelle unité, à quel concert faudrait-il s'attendre de la part d'une pareille jurisprudence, ouvrage de tant de juges et de tant de tribunaux, dont l'opinion ébranlée par les secousses révolutionnaires, serait encore si diverse-

ment modifiée ! quelle serait enfin le régulateur de cette jurisprudence disparate, qui devrait nécessairement se composer
de jugemens non sujets à cassation, puis qu'ils ne reposeraient
pas sur la base fixe des lois, mais sur des principes indéterminés d'équité, sur des usages vagues, sur des idées logiciennes, et, pour tout dire en un mot, sur l'arbitraire !

A un système incomplet de législation, serait donc joint
pour supplément une jurisprudence défectueuse.

Pour l'éviter, le législateur pourrait tourner ses vues sur
son propre ouvrage, le compléter lui-même autant que possible, et ne considérer le projet de Code que comme *les Institutes du droit français*, à l'instar des institutes de JUSTINIEN
à l'égard du droit romain. Comme ces dernières, le projet de
Code contiendrait les principes généraux du droit, et, pour
ainsi dire, le texte des lois. Le commentaire, le développe-
ment et les détails sur chaque matière devraient être l'objet
de tout autant de traités séparés, comme ils le sont à-peu-près
dans le Code et dans le Digeste du droit romain.

Une autre methode pourrait peut-être conduire le législateur à un résultat non moins heureux, quoiqu'avec moins
d'effort, de travail et de secousses ; si l'unité, dans le système
législatif, est d'une utilité si évidente qu'elle doit être envi-
sagée comme un dogme politique dont il ne peut pas être
permis de s'écarter, il est certain aussi que la France, telle
qu'elle est aujourd'hui, est un état trop étendu pour que la
différence des climats n'en nécessite une dans certaines lois,
que la nature des choses et celle du sol modifient nécessairement.

Ainsi, *laisser subsister les différences locales* en tout ce qu'elles
ne choquent pas l'esprit général et *ramener le reste à l'uni-
formité,* telle paraît être la tâche du législateur.

Pour atteindre ce but, faut-il tout détruire, abroger toutes
les lois anciennes pour tout récréer ? Il paraît plus simple
et plus naturel de maintenir l'ancien système, en y dérogeant
sur les points qui doivent être ramenés à l'unité et à l'uni-
formité, et sur-tout ceux dont notre nouvelle situation politique demande la modification ou la réforme.

Quant à ces deniers points, l'ouvrage paraît déjà porté à

sa perfection dans le livre premier du projet du Code, sur l'état des personnes, et dans les différentes lois rendues par nos assemblées nationales.

A l'égard des autres points, sur lesquels doivent tomber le changement et la réforme nécessités par l'unité du système, il semble qu'on ne peut pas s'y méprendre, et qu'ils ne se présentent pas en si grand nombre. En effet, en laissant de côté toutes les dispositions ou principes du droit naturel, appelés *la raison écrite*, dont l'équité évidente s'allie avec tous les systêmes législatifs, il ne resterait précisement que les points de droit ou les matières que nous avons appelés plus haut *systematiques*, parce que leur règle est moins dans l'invariable nature que dans la variable combinaison des convenances particulières et générales.

D'apres ce plan, qui paraît si simple, les matières à traiter dans le nouveau Code se réduiraient à-peu près *à la puissance paternelle, et aux obligations des pères envers leurs enfans; aux tutelles, minorités, et interdictions, aux successions et aux donations entre-vifs, ou à cause de mort, aux droits des époux dans les contrats de mariage, aux hypothèques, aux ventes forcées, et aux prescriptions.*

Toutes les autres matières pourraient ainsi rester à leur place, et avec leur force dans le dépôt des anciennes lois; et ces lois, soit générales, soit particulières ou locales, continueraient d'être exécutées comme auparavant dans tout ce qui n'y aurait pas été dérogé par la loi nouvelle du Code.

Cette méthode pourrait réunir les deux objets d'importance majeure que le législateur doit avoit principalement en vue, l'utilité générale de l'unité du système avec les convenances particulières des localités. Ainsi, le contact des lois anciennes et nouvelles dans un nombre de points infiniment moindres, faciliterait davantage leur cohérence et leur liaison. Avec beaucoup moins d'efforts, la législation serait plus complète et la jurisprudence plus certaine. La règle ne manquerait pas au juge, et la contravention aux lois aurait un correctif. Au lieu de détruire, on ne ferait, pour ainsi dire, que réparer, et le changement paraîtrait moins une innovation qu'une conservation de ce qu'il n'est pas nécessaire de détruire, et une amélioration de ce qu'il est utile de réformer ou de modifier.

Tel paraît être le modèle du Code que réclame la situation actuelle de la France. On le croit tracé en entier dans la maxime rappelée dans le discours préliminaire du projet, où. il est dit : *Qu'il est utile de conserver tout ce qu'il n'est pas nécessaire de détruire.* En effet, les changemens dans les lois ne sauraient être trop réfléchis, et ils ne peuvent être justifiés que par une utilité évidente : *in rebus novis constituendis,* dit la loi romaine, puisée dans les écrits de Platon, *evidens debet esse utilitas ut recedatur ab eo jure quod diu æquum visum est.*

LONDON :

Printed by Littlewood & Co.
Old Bailey.